# An Introduction to
# MATERIALS

For the last decade, the Science for Conservators volumes have been the key basic texts for conservators throughout the world. Scientific concepts are fundamental to the conservation of artefacts of every type, yet many conservators have little or no scientific training. These introductory volumes provide non-scientists with the essential theoretical background to their work.

*Editor in chief*   Andrew Wheatcroft

*The Heritage: Care–Preservation–Management* programme has been designed to serve the needs of the museum and heritage community worldwide. It publishes books and information services for professional museum and heritage workers, and for all the organisations that service the museum community.

The programme has been devised with the advice and assistance of the leading institutions in the museum and heritage community, at an international level, with ICOM and ICOMOS, with the national and local museum organisations and with individual specialists drawn from every continent.

**Forward Planning:** *A handbook of business, corporate and development planning for museums and galleries*
Edited by Timothy Ambrose and Sue Runyard

**The Industrial Heritage:** *Managing resources and uses*
Judith Alfrey and Tim Putnam

**Museums 2000:** *Politics, people, professionals and profit*
Edited by Patrick Boylan

**Museums and the Shaping of Knowledge**
Eilean Hooper-Greenhill

**Museums Without Barriers:** *A new deal for disabled people*
Fondation de France and ICOM

**The Past in Contemporary Society: Then, Now**
Peter J. Fowler

**The Representation of the Past:** *Museums and heritage in the post-modern world*
Kevin Walsh

# SCIENCE FOR CONSERVATORS
## Volume 1
# An Introduction to MATERIALS
## Conservation Science Teaching Series

The Conservation Unit
of the Museums & Galleries Commission
in conjunction with Routledge
London and New York

**Scientific Editor**

Jonathan Ashley-Smith
Keeper of Conservation
Victoria & Albert Museum

**Series Editor (Books 1–3)**

Helen Wilks

**Adviser**

Graham Weaver
Senior Lecturer
Department of Materials
Science
Faculty of Technology
Open University

**Authors**

Graham Weaver
Senior Lecturer
Department of Materials Science
Faculty of Technology
Open University

Jonathan Ashley-Smith
Keeper of Conservation
Victoria & Albert Museum

Ashok Roy
Scientific Adviser
National Gallery

Sarah Staniforth
Adviser for Conservation of Paintings
The National Trust

*Also* Harold Barker
Ex-Keeper of Conservation
British Museum

**Advisers**

Suzanne Keene
Head of Collections Services Group
Science Museum

June Lennox
Ex-Director
Stained Glass Studio
Canterbury Cathedral

Janet Notman
Ex-Chief Conservator
The Burrell Collection
Glasgow

Garry Thomson
Ex-Scientific Adviser
National Gallery

First published by the Crafts Council 1982
Second impression 1984

Published by the Conservation Unit of the
Museums & Galleries Commission in 1987

New hardback and paperback edition published in 1992
by Routledge
11 New Fetter Lane, London EC4P 4EE

Simultaneously published in the USA and Canada
by Routledge
a division of Routledge, Chapman and Hall Inc.
29 West 35th Street, New York, NY 10001

© 1987, 1992 Museums & Galleries Commission

Illustrations by Berry/Fallon Design
Designed by Robert Updegraff and Gillian Crossley-Holland

Printed in England by Butler & Tanner Ltd,
Frome and London

*British Library Cataloguing in Publication Data*
A catalogue record for this book is available
from the British Library.

*Library of Congress Cataloging in Publication Data*
*applied for*

ISBN 0 415 07166 6 (hbk)
ISBN 0 415 07167 4 (pbk)

# Contents

## Preface to the 1992 edition

The science of conserving artworks and other items of cultural significance has undergone considerable change since 1982 when this series was instigated, mostly involving the development or application of new materials or techniques. Their understanding by conservators, restorers and students continues, nonetheless, to depend on familiarity with the underlying scientific principles which do not change and which are clearly explained in these books.

In response to continued international demand for this series, The Conservation Unit is pleased to be associated with Routledge in presenting these new editions as part of The Heritage: Care–Preservation–Management programme. The volumes are now enhanced by lists of recommended reading which will lead the reader to further helpful texts, developing scientific ideas in a conservation setting and bringing their application up to date.

# Introduction

The book was lying near Alice on the table . . . . . . she turned over the leaves, to find some part that she could read. "— for it's all in some language I don't know," she said to herself.

It was like this

JABBERWOCKY.

'Twas brillig, and the slithy toves
Did gyre and gimble in the wabe;
All mimsy were the borogoves,
And the mome raths outgrabe.

She puzzled over this for some time, but at last a bright thought struck her. "Why, it's a Looking-glass book, of course! And if I hold it up to a glass, the words will all go the right way again."

"It seems very pretty," she said when she had finished it, "but it's *rather* hard to understand!" (You see she didn't like to confess even to herself, that she couldn't make it out at all.) "Somehow it seems to fill my head with ideas – only I don't exactly know what they are!"

Through the Looking Glass and What Alice found there
Lewis Carroll, 1872.

Alice expresses the sentiments felt by many conservators and restorers who have a non-scientific background but are faced with the task of learning science from standard text books. It is for this reason that the Crafts Council has drawn together a team of conservation scientists, conservators and science teachers to prepare this special teaching series for your use. The series is an elementary one, assuming no previous knowledge of science, although the texts at times use words and mention conservation procedures which you already use frequently in your work. It progresses gradually, step by step, to cover the basic science which has a direct bearing on your work.

The books have been compiled to be applicable to all areas of conservation practice. This may, at first, seem unnecessary to specialist conservators, but one of the great virtues of gaining an understanding of science is the knowledge it gives you of the way the behaviour of different materials interrelates. In this way, the preoccupations of a textile conservator and a paper conservator, for example, will be seen to have much in common; less obviously a textile conservator may often find it useful to know something about the behaviour and properties of a metal thread. Many other conservators, especially in areas such as ethnography or archaeology, work with a wide range of materials and so for them the benefits of this approach are self evident.

Although they use basic conservation activities to guide you towards an understanding of some science and its uses, these books are *not* conservation manuals or handbooks. The major purpose of the series is to use the activities which are central to your work to make clear to you the relevance of science and some of the basic elements of scientific thought. This will enable you to go on to discover more for yourself from the many specialist papers and books on conservation which are already available. The Crafts Council and the team who have worked on these books also hope that their publication will facilitate and help to form a base for back-up courses and lectures in conservation science, which would give those of you reading these books without easy access to a teacher, the chance for valuable discussion and assistance.

*Using This Book*
This book, the first in a series of six, assumes no previous scientific knowledge at the start. However, as you progress through each chapter you will need to have already read and assimilated the teaching in all the preceding ones. Science tends to build up its picture one step upon another, and so if you try to read a later section in advance of others, you will run the risk of becoming very confused, or else of only partially grasping its meaning.

Remember that Book I is not a complete scientific course in itself. It will be necessary to read Books II, III, etc. before a useful syllabus is built up. You may also find that the order of this book (and the others in the series) varies slightly from more standard science text books but this is because the text is structured to suit the specific needs of practising conservators.

Book I provides you with a very basic introduction to the language of science and to the scientific approach. It takes you through some crucial elementary steps towards being able to identify materials in scientific terms and introduces you to basic chemistry. Gradually, as the series moves on, the science taught in this book will be developed further, as the science behind different conservation procedures is discussed. The final chapter of this first book in the series will also provide you with a useful guide to the chemical names frequently encountered in conservation, showing how their chemical properties are related to their structures.

When reading this book, allow yourself to become completely familiar with a section and confident about its contents before moving on to the next. Do not read large portions at any one sitting. Although the series *is* an elementary one, you will need to take plenty of time in working all the way through it. You should not feel disheartened if your progress at times seems slow. If you *do* have particular difficulty with a section, ask a scientist or another conservator with a knowledge of science about it. It is not worth struggling on your own; even a scientist with no knowledge of conservation can help. Very often the problem seems surprisingly simple to clear away if you can go through it with somebody else.

Worked examples and exercises have been included where they will be useful. Check your answers at the back of the book. Occasionally, some simple demonstrations are suggested to illustrate or clarify the written text. At relevant points you will also find reference tables and as scientific words appear or are defined for the first time, they are printed in bold type (as well as appearing in the outer margins) for easy reference. A full index is included at the end of the book.

*Acknowledgements*

This book has been prepared by a team of conservation scientists, conservators and science teachers. The Crafts Council is deeply grateful to the conservators, and in particular the conservation scientists, who, as authors, have given an enormous amount of their own time to this project over the last three years. The Council also wishes to acknowledge the generosity of the institutions and private workshops (in particular the National Gallery, the Victoria and Albert Museum and the Open University), who have lent their support through allowing their staff to work with us. The contributions made to such a complex and difficult educational task have been necessarily varied but each has been of great value and importance. The Council is especially indebted to Jonathan Ashley-Smith, who has contributed so much as scientific editor.

July 1982

1

# What science is

A   The value of science
B   Identifying materials
C   Levels of identity
D   The use of instruments and scientific language
E   Observations and theories
F   Measurement and accuracy in practice

---

# What science is

Science is a systematic and structured way of understanding the material world. Scientists aim to describe material facts in an objective manner. To help fulfil this aim, they have developed a precise language and a specialist vocabulary to describe accurately what they have learnt from their observations. Scientific ideas and theories are continually evolving, and being revised (though by no means at an even or steady pace), as further observations and new discoveries are made.

Scientists have assimilated this language and mode of expression and use it to develop their own researches further. Science enables you to understand and link phenomena which might, on the face of it, appear problematic and unconnected. Conservators, therefore, can find this precise and structured way of looking at the material world both helpful and illuminating. This book and the subsequent ones will introduce you gradually to the language of science, especially as it relates to the work of the conservator.

# *A* The value of science

The insight which science can bring to you, the conservator, will provide a greater confidence in choosing a suitable course of action when treating an object. It will help you to understand more about the historic materials you work on and also the many other materials you use during conservation treatment. This understanding is bound to be useful when you consider the many new materials which are continually being introduced. It is important for you as a conservator to evaluate these new developments carefully yourself. It is a great advantage to be able to read the many published articles, which discuss new methods and materials, with some confidence in your own ability to understand the science behind the discussion. As a conservator you are naturally cautious. Scientific understanding can help you choose sensible ways of proceeding when a problem is posed. It can help you to organise tests of new materials more satisfactorily and to select preventative conservation measures. Not least, science can help you to be more aware of safety in the workshop and laboratory, both for yourself and for the objects you work on.

Nevertheless, to the experienced conservator, who has gathered considerable practical knowledge and skill over the years, the **scientific approach** may sometimes appear laborious or simplistic. A conservator used to working with metal may feel able to judge intuitively how much pressure a bent object will take in order to straighten it without being damaged. A scientist, however, given the same problem, but lacking the same practical experience, might approach the task very differently. The scientist would want to identify the metal of which the object was made, and would use analytical equipment to provide data about the composition of the metal. The scientist would look up what was known about the strengths of such material and, after measuring the thickness of metal, might be able to calculate the exact force required to straighten the bent object. The calculations might also give some indication of the safety margin; the extra amount of force that would cause the metal to snap. With the right equipment the predetermined force could be applied in a controlled manner and the piece would be straightened.

The conservator goes through the same processes of identifying, drawing on existing knowledge, and applying a controlled force and so, in an unconscious way, is being equally scientific. The main difference is that the scientist would have used an approach that relied on measurement and numbers. In this simple example the scientist would not have been able to offer much help to the conservator. There are many other occasions, however, where a conservator's practical judgement through sight, touch and past experience, may be inadequate. For example, a conservator once received a metal object which was encrusted with mud. It was described as pewter, and he accepted this description because of its

**scientific approach**

appearance and feel. After washing off the mud, he placed the object to dry in an oven at 105°C, and to his horror it melted. Later chemical analysis, coupled with the object's lack of provenance, established it as a modern fake made from an alloy with a very low melting point. The fear of experiencing this type of disaster must be present in the mind of every conservator. It is important to be able to judge when and how science can be of use to you.

# *B* Identifying materials

Everyone from very early childhood develops the ability to recognise and identify materials and objects. Amongst conservators this skill tends to become very highly developed. It is needed because to know what an object is made of is a fundamental preliminary to diagnosing its condition and deciding on a method of treatment. Often **identification** seems to occur as an instinctive and almost instantaneous process. The process, however, is worth looking at in greater detail.

    Pick up any object which comes immediately to hand (you may choose an object you are working on, or something in your workshop – a tool perhaps, or a domestic article – it won't matter what). By using your senses such as touch, sight and smell, and your experience, decide what it is made of. In making your decisions pay special attention to *how* you arrive at your conclusions. Look at, for example, the process and reasoning behind identifying the materials in a simple and familiar object. Suppose you had picked up a chisel and identified it as having a steel blade and a wooden handle bound by a brass collar. *How* you did this is an interesting (though simple) exercise in the process of identification. The starting point was to recognise the *function* of the object. Because the blade was shiny, hard and cold to touch you knew, by comparison with past memories, that it was "metal". You automatically rejected the idea of the metal being silver or aluminium – it was too rigid, had the wrong shininess and did not feel the right weight for those metals. Also, from experience, you *knew* that steel is the best material for cutting-tools and therefore *expected* the blade to be steel. Similarly the handle *looked* like wood (colour, grain) and *felt* like wood (warm to touch, texture, weight). The yellow metal collar just had to be brass – gold, the other yellow metal, is too expensive to use on a functional object.

    With your actual example, which may have been more complex, you will have gone through a similar routine to narrow the field: first a judgement of the function and possible age of the object and perhaps evidence of how it was made. Comparison with your previous experience of, say, which materials were used for particular purposes in different historical periods begins to generate *expectations* of what the materials are. Stylistic information may also give clues to where the object came from and when it was made.

**identification**

**Figure 1.1**   *This chart shows the groups of readily identifiable materials, and the levels of investigation necessary for complete identification. The two broad classes of matter (organic and inorganic) are related to the original sources of the materials.*

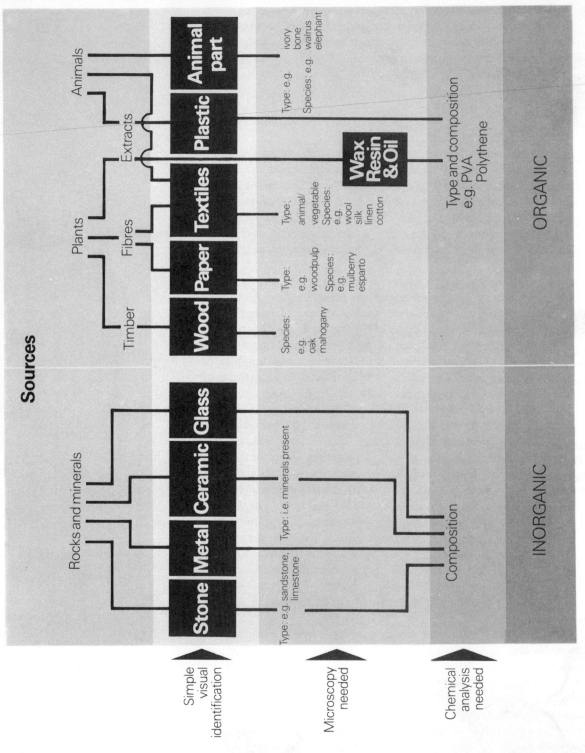

# C Levels of identity

The process of identification, described in the previous section, used only the simplest methods. Take a look at the chart (Figure 1.1). At the level marked "simple visual identification" there are nine broad classes of material. It is easy to classify a material as one of these, because each class has a distinctive combination of such properties as colour, texture, density and rigidity. Your visual and tactile senses are brought to bear on the problem and you relate what you see to the properties of materials you know.

When you identify an object as belonging to one of these categories you are also saying that you *expect* it to show certain properties that have been observed in other objects in the same class. For instance, you might expect all objects in one category to deteriorate in much the same manner. The idea that you *expect* one member of a class to behave in much the same way as the others is similar to the approach adopted by scientists. By making detailed observations and measurements they are able to obtain more information about the properties of a group. These investigations lead to more detailed classifications.

For many conservation problems, the *level* of description needs to be refined far beyond that of "stone", "metal" or "wood". The degree of refinement is dictated by the particular conservation task and the nature of the material. For instance, it may be required to know the exact species of wood in a piece of furniture, so that a missing piece of veneer can be replaced or so that the authenticity of the piece can be assessed. It has been discovered that all types of wood are basically similar in their material content, so it is not very useful to examine the chemical constituents of a sample of timber if you want to identify a particular species. What is needed is a close look at the cell structure (as a thin specimen under the microscope) which will reveal all that is necessary to identify it. The fibres in different types of paper or textile can be similarly recognised, by their distinctive fine structures which can be seen clearly under the microscope. **Microscopy** is shown as the next level of investigation after simple visual identification. It is quite sufficient for the exact identification of a whole range of materials. It distinguishes the many types of animal and plant product and often may be used to identify the species. At the microscopic level, paint media and adhesives can be seen as different from the main body of the object, which is why the class of resins, oils and waxes has been placed below the simple visual level. However, these products cannot be identified with the microscope alone. This brings us to the more subtle level of identification labelled **chemical analysis.**

For instance, you might need to know the exact nature (the chemical composition) of a corrosion product on the surface of a metal artefact in order to be sure of a safe removal procedure and subsequent safe environmental conditions for the object. This would involve identifying both the metal and its alteration product by

**microscopy**

**chemical analysis**

chemical analysis. To recognise something as made of iron or lead or copper is, in essence, a *chemical* identification; the actual substance itself is being defined. On the whole, such identifications cannot be made just by looking, even under the microscope. Some characteristic unique to the material must be exploited; this may be done by a chemical test. The same applies when you need to know the exact composition of something. Glass, for example, is easy to recognise as a class of material from its superficial properties. Of course not all glass is the same; a great variety of composition is possible. Different forms of glass can be made from a range of starting materials. Under the microscope the different types are not in the least characteristic and so, should a type of glass need to be identified, a full chemical analysis might be required. Alternatively, a partial analysis may be all that is necessary, say to determine the proportion of lead present.

Identification may take the form of description (as with wood, paper or natural textiles), or chemical analysis of composition (eg glass, ceramics, metal), and sometimes a combination of the two. Often what you know about the origins or function of an object will be of great help in narrowing the field of choice in deciding what it might be made of; the more complicated (and rigorous) tests of microscopical examination or chemical testing can then be applied in the light of what you know. For example, you would not expect an Italian Renaissance painting to be on a mahogany panel, nor would you expect an Anglo-Saxon sword-blade to be made of chrome steel. The first example would require an identification at the level of wood species (by microscopy); the second a chemical identification to identify the composition of the metal blade.

Having looked at the means of making increasingly specific and detailed identifications and analyses of materials, look again at the chart and in particular at the two large rectangles marked **inorganic** and **organic**. You will perhaps already be familiar with the idea that stone, metal, ceramics and glass are all derived from rocks and/or minerals and are termed *inorganic*. The idea that wood, paper, and many textiles are derived directly from plants, while wool, silk, leather, fur and bones are all animal products will also be straightforward enough. Referring again to the chart you will see that they all appear within the rectangle marked *organic*. What may well appear as more surprising, however, is that many **synthetic** (artificial) **materials** (eg all plastics, PVA, polythene, etc.), made from extracted chemicals derived from animal and plant products, are also termed organic. (Do not forget that many substances, although looking deceptively like inorganic materials are, of course, derived from animals or plants. Coal and fuel oil are both derived from fossilised plants and animals.) There are, too, both natural and artificial inorganic materials. For example, the pigment vermilion can occur naturally as the mineral cinnabar and can also be manufactured from mercury and sulphur. The two forms are chemically identical.

The terms *organic* and *inorganic* distinguish two groups of material with different sources. This division by source is shown at the top of Figure 1.1. You might expect that there would be an

*inorganic organic*

*synthetic materials*

equally obvious distinction to be discovered by the investigation of chemical composition. This turns out to be the case. The words *organic* and *inorganic* as chemical descriptions will start to have greater meaning as your appreciation of material in chemical terms increases.

## *D* The use of instruments and scientific language

The fact that your own methodical approach to your work is "scientific" may be obscured for you by an idea that scientists are different in some way from other people. People without scientific training naturally notice that "science" involves the use of apparently strange instruments and an apparently foreign language. You may well feel, quite subconsciously, that "scientists" are much more intelligent than you are, or that their brains work in a different way, or that they are operating a kind of intellectual "closed shop". None of these feelings represents any sort of truth. The use of highly specific instruments comes about from the need to make observations on a very minute level; the use of "obscure" language from the need to describe what has been observed or discovered. In the previous section, more complex ways of identifying materials were suggested and these tended to imply the use of instruments or else a knowledge of chemistry. It was suggested that you might, for example, use a microscope to extend your powers of vision when identifying paper or wood.

The use of instruments is obviously not restricted to identification. If you wished to maintain correct storage conditions for an object, you would need, amongst other things, to monitor the temperature of its environment and you would use a thermometer. The use of this instrument provides a greater accuracy than merely feeling whether the room is warm or cool. The thermometer offers you a **measurement** of the room temperature in degrees.

**measurement**

Because all scientific thought and activity is based on making detailed observations, scientists have needed to develop and use instruments of varying complexity as a means of measuring and then interpreting what they have observed. Instruments often relay the information they are designed to detect in terms of numbers, for instance the number of degrees marked on the thermometer. Other examples are a rule marked off in cm and mm or a pH meter which indicates acidity or alkalinity in terms of a 1–14 scale.

It will be quite obvious to you that your work as a conservator can depend on the correct use of instruments (of many different kinds and for differing purposes) and on your ability to use them appropriately and safely. The information which an instrument may offer is usually limited in kind although instruments are normally able to detect and quantify far beyond the ability of unaided human senses. It is partly for this reason that much of the data they give can appear rather abstract or obscure, particularly as many of the

**scientific language**

phenomena described by scientists are only detectable with the aid of instruments. To describe things that are not obviously a part of the everyday world of the senses, new words have been created and these have been incorporated into a **scientific language**.

Every new discovery (not only in the field of science) has meant that new words have had to be created or old words given specific meanings, to describe what was previously unknown. The language scientists use may at first appear almost foreign. However, it has a regularity and pattern which, once several fundamental scientific ideas have been understood, makes it far more consistent and comprehensible than might at first appear. The scientific language, like the instruments you use, is aimed at providing a precise and accurate means of describing the phenomena investigated by scientists. This means that as you read the books in this series, you will find that certain words, used freely within normal conversation (for example, words like *radical, buffer, reaction, stress*) have a very specific meaning within a scientific context. Other words (such as *carbon dioxide*) will tell you something about the substance itself, once you have begun to understand a little about chemistry. Others still (such as *esters, isotopes,* and *polymerisation*) are found in the language of science alone. Along with the new words there are also **symbolic representations**, and these are especially prevalent in chemistry. These symbols are often combined to form equations, designed as shorthand notation to describe chemical processes. It is hoped that by the end of the series your understanding of the language and vocabulary of science will be sufficient for you to read most technical articles on conservation subjects with some understanding of the scientific principles involved.

**symbolic representations**

# *E* Observations and theories

It is a common misconception that science represents incontrovertible truth. While science *is* concerned to represent facts on the basis of consistent observation as objectively as possible, the scientist has to look for *a way of describing* what has been observed. Because scientists are always aware that their descriptions of phenomena are often only visualisations of what cannot be seen but they believe must exist in reality, they often prefer, when describing something, to refer to their description as a **model** for understanding it. This word reminds one that science is not a series of static or absolute statements about the material world, but rather a framework by which to understand it. It is a continually evolving process that is constantly being revised and developed further as more observations are made.

**model**

The scientific way of thinking and acting is, at root, simply an extension of natural common sense, curiosity and intelligence. It relies on our predilection for observing situations and occurrences and our ability to detect patterns and connections within them. Consistent observation of a particular pattern of events may lead the observer to devise a **theory** (a statement of what is likely to be true, arrived at through detailed observation and experiment) to explain the consistency. This theory may then be tested by an experiment or by further observations. If observations and experiments suggest that a particular occurrence is always, without exception, accompanied by a particular pattern of consequences, this may be stated as a "**law**". A scientific law does not dictate to nature what will happen, on the contrary it says that "because this has always been observed to be the case, it probably always will be".

The relationship of observation and theory, hypothesis and experiment can be illustrated using the example of the fading of textiles in light. An observant person might see that some curtains had faded quite badly and that the cloth was falling apart. By making further simple observations this person notices, too, that other window curtains fade and deteriorate and that carpets and upholstery also near the windows fade rapidly, although tapestries and tablecloths further away from them are not so badly affected. What do the faded textiles have in common? The observations are sufficient to suggest an idea (hypothesis) that there is a connection between daylight and the fading and decay of textiles. The observed changes cannot be due to handling, as a frequently used tablecloth, for example, has not suffered so badly. It cannot be the difference in temperature between the window and the middle of the room because a chair in front of the window has faded but one right next to it in the shadow has hardly changed. The idea that fading is related to light falling on the material is only a **hypothesis** (a surmised truth on which to base further reasoning) until the relationship has been proved. It could be proved by making a large number of observations to confirm that where textiles are kept in light they always fade but when they are stored in the dark they never do. Alternatively, it could be confirmed by a controlled experiment in which a textile is deliberately placed partly in light and partly in shadow and the different reactions observed.

The observer may also develop more complicated hypotheses – that the amount of decay depends on the quantity of light that has fallen on the material, or that light of one colour causes more damage than another. These hypotheses are best verified by **controlled experiments** in which the variables such as light intensity, duration of exposure and colour change can be accurately measured.

To help his or her own understanding and in an attempt to explain these observations to others, the experimenter may develop a theory of the fading of textiles by light. This theory will combine the observations, the results of the experiments and any hypotheses about the nature of light or the chemistry of the textiles which, although necessary to the theory, cannot be proved at that time.

The value of a theory is that it can be used to predict how a particular substance will behave in a particular situation. However, the only way to *know* what will happen is to do the experiment and make the observations. Thomas Huxley refers to "The great tragedy of Science – the slaying of a beautiful hypothesis by an ugly fact."

**theory**

**law**

**hypothesis**

**controlled experiments**

## F Measurement and accuracy in practice

Through reading the previous sections it will have become increasingly clear to you how much science relies on making disciplined and accurate observations. Many scientific observations are based on measurement, although some require the use of sophisticated and expensive instruments. Generally speaking these specialised facilities need trained personnel both to work the machines and to assess their appropriateness in any application. Conservation workshops will rarely be equipped with these machines and so conservators will probably only have access to them through consultation with others. This is probably no great disadvantage for the greater part as, normally, much more modest techniques can adequately solve most practical conservation problems. But whether "high technology" science or simple methods are used, there is always a need to understand and use sound experimental techniques.

**experimental technique**

"Sound **experimental technique**" describes a systematic and well informed approach to the factors which may affect any practical work being undertaken. In a conservation workshop it could, for example, be measuring out the correct weight of substances in order to ensure that they form a solution of the right strength for a particular job. It could mean obtaining an accurate reading using a pH meter (see Book II). It might involve conducting some tests in a manner that will produce helpful and reliable results, such as testing whether the dyes in a textile will run when it is washed.

There are, of course, many instances where it will be difficult for you to know exhaustively *all* the variable factors that may affect your practical work. However, just as you would guard against accident by ensuring that an object is placed in a safe position on your workbench, so common sense and an understanding of science will show that there are several fundamental and often quite straightforward factors to be considered. It will gradually become less difficult for you to judge what these are likely to be in a given situation as your understanding of basic science develops. Once you are able to judge the variables likely to affect the results of your work, and when you are able to understand *why* they do, you will then have the means to find ways of controlling them.

### Measuring relative humidity

The measurement of *relative humidity* (RH) has been chosen to illustrate this systematic approach to practical work, because it will be familiar to most conservators and because the factors affecting its measurement are quite simple to control.

Ask yourself the following questions:
1  What *is* humidity?
2  Why do I need to know about humidity?
3  What causes changes in humidity?
4  What does the special term '*relative* humidity' mean?

 5  How is RH measured and are there any calculations involved?
 6  How do the measuring instruments work?
 7  How accurate do the measurements have to be?
 8  What affects the accuracy of the measurements?
 9  How do the inaccuracies show up?
10  How can inaccuracies be prevented or kept to a minimum?

All these questions are answered to some extent below, though not necessarily in the order they were asked.

*Relative humidity*

It has been found, through long observation, that the majority of objects conservators work on are affected by the amount of water in the atmosphere in one way or another. In damp conditions metal objects may corrode and mould will grow on organic materials like paper or glue. When the air is excessively dry furniture may crack and veneer lift from its backing. Even more damaging are actual *changes* in humidity, when materials expand as the humidity rises and contract as it falls. An object that contains several different materials which each respond differently to changes in humidity can warp and the materials separate, causing considerable damage. This makes it important to be able to control humidity and the first step in doing that is to be able to measure it.

**Humidity** is the amount of water held as a vapour in air. It is expressed as the weight of water in a given volume of air. This measurement is called the **absolute humidity** and is usually given as the number of grams of water vapour in a cubic metre of air (written as $g/m^3$). **humidity**  **absolute humidity**

In conservation, however, it is **relative** humidity that is important. Air at two different temperatures may have the same absolute humidity and yet have very different effects on moisture-sensitive objects. Air at 30°C containing $10g/m^3$ of water causes an object to dry out, yet if this air is cooled to 10°C condensation could occur on the object's surface. **relative humidity**

Relative humidity, as the name implies, is an expression of one humidity measurement *relative* to another. The two measurements are:

i  the *actual* amount of water vapour in a given volume of air at a particular temperature; and

ii  the *maximum* amount of water that the same volume of air can hold at the same temperature.

The actual amount is expressed as a percentage of the maximum amount.

At 30°C the maximum weight of water that air can hold as vapour is $17g/m^3$. Suppose the actual weight of water present is only $10g/m^3$. We need to express 10 as a percentage of 17 to get a figure for the RH. To do this we divide 10 by 17 and multiply by 100 (easy enough with a pocket calculator).

$$RH = \frac{10}{17} \times 100 = 59\%$$

**hygrometers**

**recording hygrograph**

The simplest methods of measuring RH rely on the expansion and contraction of a moisture-sensitive material as the RH rises and falls. **Hygrometers** (see Figure 1.2) containing elements of paper or hair are the most commonly used instruments for measuring RH. The needle moves as a paper strip or bundle of hairs expands and contracts.

A more sophisticated instrument, the **recording hygrograph** (Figure 1.3) can be used to keep a record of RH over a period of time, usually one week. The bundle of hairs contracts as the RH falls and by a series of levers pulls the pen down on the chart which is slowly rotating. The pen rises as the hairs expand with rising RH. However,

**Figure 1.2** *Two hygrometers. Left, a paper hygrometer, which shows the paper coil; right, a hair hygrometer. Both would need calibrating against a psychometric instrument.*

**Figure 1.3** *Thermohygrograph. This instrument usually records both temperature and relative humidity.*

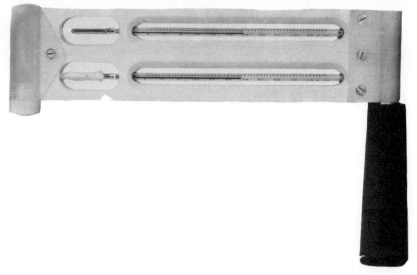

**Figure 1.4**  *Sling psychrometer (sometimes called a whirling hygrometer).*

both the paper hygrometers and the recording hygrograph slowly
begin to give inaccurate readings and have to be adjusted to read
correctly again. This adjustment is called **calibration** and it requires
a measurement of RH from some other source that is known to be
consistently accurate. The slow drift away from accuracy is caused
by the moisture-sensitive element losing its elasticity and becoming
stretched, and so failing to return to its original tautness after expansion. Used on their own these instruments are useless. They must be
calibrated using a second, more accurate instrument.

    A **psychrometer** is generally used, the most familiar being
the sling psychrometer. It relies on the cooling effect observed when
water evaporates. The drier the air, the faster the water will
evaporate and the greater the cooling effect will be. In a psychrometer two identical thermometers are fixed side by side. The bulb
of one of them is surrounded by a fabric sleeve that is moistened with
distilled water. This is called the wet bulb; the other is called the dry
bulb. The evaporation of the water from the wet bulb is accelerated
by passing a current of air over it. This is achieved by whirling the
instrument. The drier the air, the lower the wet bulb temperature
will be compared with the dry.

    After reading the two thermometers the wet bulb temperature is
subtracted from the dry bulb temperature to give what is called the
*depression* of the wet bulb. Using this figure and the dry bulb temperature the RH can be looked up in a chart (Figure 1.5). The column
on the left is the dry bulb temperature and the row across the top
is the difference between the wet and dry bulb temperatures. The
RH is read by following along the line from the dry bulb temperature
until the column for the appropriate temperature difference is
reached.

**calibration**

**psychrometer**

If the dry bulb temperature is 22°C and the wet bulb temperature is $17\frac{1}{2}$°C the difference between these two is $4\frac{1}{2}$°C. On the table it can be seen that the RH corresponding to a dry bulb temperature of 22°C and a depression of wet bulb of $4\frac{1}{2}$°C is 64%.

| Dry Bulb (°C) | Depression of the wet bulb (°C) | | | | | | | | | | | | | |
|---|---|---|---|---|---|---|---|---|---|---|---|---|---|---|
| | 0 | $\frac{1}{2}$ | 1 | $1\frac{1}{2}$ | 2 | $2\frac{1}{2}$ | 3 | $3\frac{1}{2}$ | 4 | $4\frac{1}{2}$ | 5 | $5\frac{1}{2}$ | 6 | $6\frac{1}{2}$ | 7 |
| 40 | 100 | 97 | 94 | 91 | 88 | 85 | 82 | 80 | 77 | 74 | 72 | 69 | 67 | 64 | 62 |
| 39 | 100 | 97 | 94 | 91 | 88 | 85 | 82 | 79 | 77 | 74 | 71 | 69 | 66 | 64 | 61 |
| 38 | 100 | 97 | 94 | 91 | 88 | 85 | 82 | 79 | 76 | 74 | 71 | 68 | 66 | 63 | 61 |
| 37 | 100 | 97 | 94 | 91 | 87 | 85 | 82 | 79 | 76 | 73 | 70 | 68 | 65 | 63 | 60 |
| 36 | 100 | 97 | 94 | 90 | 87 | 84 | 81 | 78 | 76 | 73 | 70 | 67 | 65 | 62 | 60 |
| 35 | 100 | 97 | 93 | 90 | 87 | 84 | 81 | 78 | 75 | 72 | 70 | 67 | 64 | 61 | 59 |
| 34 | 100 | 97 | 93 | 90 | 87 | 84 | 81 | 78 | 75 | 72 | 69 | 66 | 64 | 61 | 58 |
| 33 | 100 | 97 | 93 | 90 | 87 | 83 | 80 | 77 | 74 | 71 | 69 | 66 | 63 | 60 | 58 |
| 32 | 100 | 97 | 93 | 90 | 86 | 83 | 80 | 77 | 74 | 71 | 68 | 65 | 62 | 60 | 57 |
| 31 | 100 | 96 | 93 | 90 | 86 | 83 | 80 | 77 | 73 | 70 | 67 | 64 | 62 | 59 | 56 |
| 30 | 100 | 96 | 93 | 89 | 86 | 83 | 79 | 76 | 73 | 70 | 67 | 64 | 61 | 58 | 55 |
| 29 | 100 | 96 | 93 | 89 | 86 | 82 | 79 | 76 | 72 | 69 | 66 | 63 | 60 | 57 | 54 |
| 28 | 100 | 96 | 93 | 89 | 86 | 82 | 79 | 75 | 72 | 69 | 65 | 62 | 59 | 56 | 53 |
| 27 | 100 | 96 | 92 | 89 | 85 | 82 | 78 | 75 | 71 | 68 | 65 | 62 | 59 | 55 | 52 |
| 26 | 100 | 96 | 92 | 88 | 85 | 81 | 78 | 74 | 71 | 67 | 64 | 61 | 58 | 55 | 51 |
| 25 | 100 | 96 | 92 | 88 | 84 | 81 | 77 | 74 | 70 | 67 | 63 | 60 | 57 | 54 | 50 |
| $24\frac{1}{2}$ | 100 | 96 | 92 | 88 | 84 | 81 | 77 | 74 | 70 | 66 | 63 | 60 | 57 | 53 | 50 |
| 24 | 100 | 96 | 92 | 88 | 84 | 80 | 77 | 73 | 69 | 66 | 62 | 59 | 56 | 52 | 49 |
| $23\frac{1}{2}$ | 100 | 96 | 92 | 88 | 84 | 80 | 77 | 73 | 69 | 65 | 62 | 59 | 56 | 52 | 49 |
| 23 | 100 | 96 | 92 | 88 | 84 | 80 | 76 | 72 | 69 | 65 | 62 | 58 | 55 | 51 | 48 |
| $22\frac{1}{2}$ | 100 | 96 | 92 | 87 | 83 | 80 | 76 | 72 | 68 | 64 | 61 | 58 | 55 | 51 | 47 |
| 22 | 100 | 96 | 92 | 87 | 83 | 79 | 76 | 72 | 68 | 64 | 61 | 57 | 54 | 50 | 47 |
| $21\frac{1}{2}$ | 100 | 96 | 91 | 87 | 83 | 79 | 76 | 71 | 67 | 63 | 60 | 57 | 53 | 50 | 46 |
| 21 | 100 | 96 | 91 | 87 | 83 | 79 | 75 | 71 | 67 | 63 | 60 | 56 | 52 | 49 | 46 |
| $20\frac{1}{2}$ | 100 | 96 | 91 | 87 | 83 | 79 | 75 | 71 | 67 | 62 | 59 | 56 | 51 | 49 | 45 |
| 20 | 100 | 96 | 91 | 87 | 83 | 78 | 74 | 70 | 66 | 62 | 59 | 55 | 51 | 48 | 44 |
| $19\frac{1}{2}$ | 100 | 96 | 91 | 87 | 82 | 78 | 74 | 70 | 66 | 61 | 58 | 55 | 51 | 47 | 44 |
| 19 | 100 | 95 | 91 | 86 | 82 | 78 | 74 | 70 | 65 | 61 | 58 | 54 | 50 | 46 | 43 |

**Figure 1.5** *Portion of the psychrometric conversion chart.*

To use a psychrometer correctly, that is, to obtain accurate experimental information from it, certain precautions must be taken. The most common mistake is to have too high a wet bulb reading. This gives too high a value for the RH. If the dry bulb temperature is 22°C and the wet bulb reads 16°C instead of 15°C then the RH will be calculated as 54% instead of 47%.

Experimental carelessnesses that can lead to high wet bulb readings include:

a not whirling for long enough to allow the air to flow over the wet bulb before reading the thermometer;

b too long a pause after whirling before reading the wet bulb thermometer;

c breathing over either thermometer or putting warm hands on them;

d allowing the wick to get dirty or not using distilled water, which reduce the amount of water evaporating off the wet bulb.

Thus, in order to obtain a reliable measurement of RH it is important to use the psychrometer correctly, and this means understanding how it works. This is a vital principle in any experimental technique.

To improve the accuracy of the experiment the thermometers could be read to the nearest $\frac{1}{4}$°C rather than the nearest $\frac{1}{2}$°C as shown on the psychrometric chart (Figure 1.5). It can be seen from the table that there are quite large jumps in RH between one column and the next. For example, if the dry bulb temperature is $19\frac{1}{2}$°C and the wet bulb reads $15\frac{1}{4}$°C then the difference in temperature is $4\frac{1}{4}$°C. The RH reading for a temperature difference of 4°C is 66% and for $4\frac{1}{2}$°C is 61%. A value of RH half way between 66% and 61%, that is $63\frac{1}{2}$%, would be more accurate. If the thermometers in the psychrometer can only be read to the nearest $\frac{1}{2}$°C then the accuracy of the experiment will be limited to within $2\frac{1}{2}$% RH.

An experimental accuracy of within $2\frac{1}{2}$% of the true value may be acceptable. Fluctuations in RH of this order may not have any serious effect on furniture. If conditions for the storage of metal objects have to be maintained below 40% RH a reading of 35% is definitely safe, but one of 39% may not be. However, hygrometers that give values that are too low or too high by as much as 10% RH are quite unacceptable.

Accuracy of measurement is important in a great deal of practical conservation work, but so too is knowledge of when accuracy is needed. For example, there are certain cleaning solutions that you must use at an exact concentration, but there may be others in which the concentration is not so critical. If you were washing a delicate piece of historic costume it would be necessary to weigh accurately the ingredients for the cleaning solution. It is important that no residue remains in the textile and rinsing must be kept to the minimum, as the more the object is handled, the greater is the risk of damage. However, it is not so important to measure precisely the amount of detergent that you add to the water when you clean your overalls. You will be better able to make this sort of decision, and to see the reason behind it, when you have acquired a basic knowledge of chemistry.

**2**

# Beginning chemistry

A    Chemical names
B    Elements and compounds
C    Atoms and molecules
D    Solids, liquids and gases
E    Mixtures and purity
F    Physical and chemical changes
G    How chemical reactions happen

# Beginning chemistry

The first chapter introduced you in a general way to the structured way of thinking that science uses, showing you that in many instances this is much the same as the normal common sense approach used in conservation work. This chapter introduces the atomic theory at a simplified level, and shows how it can be used to interpret several commonplace phenomena.

## A  Chemical names

The words that are used to describe a material or a substance can give a great deal of information about its nature or they may tell us very little. The name "Jane Smith" may identify one person within a group, the word "conservator" may describe how she spends her time but we need words like animal, mammal, human and protein to give us more and more specific information about the structure and composition of Jane Smith, conservator.

If we say "stone", this word refers to a whole class of materials that have recognisable properties of hardness and density and have a common provenance. The name "marble" defines a narrower group within this class, but there is nothing in the name that helps predict a relationship with any other group of rocks. However, the name "calcium carbonate" describes marble in such a way that someone with a little knowledge of chemistry but no practical knowledge of marble or limestone could make reaonable predictions about the way both would react to acid cleaning or be affected by acidic air pollution.

**function name**

Many different kinds of name are used by conservators and by scientists. There are, for example, names that describe classes of materials. Amongst these will be those that describe the **function** of the material, such as *thinner*. Although people who use paints, lacquers and solvents will know what "thinners" do, the name doesn't indicate what thinners are made of, or even whether all thinners are the same. It doesn't enable users to look up toxicity or flammability data or to record their work with such accuracy that someone else could exactly repeat the procedure on another occasion. Other function names are *bleach, detergent, enzyme*. Another type of class name is the **commercial name**. An example is *Araldite*, which describes a range of products whose composition is presumably exactly known by the manufacturer. However, the user only knows that it is some kind of "epoxy resin", with no indication of why or how it hardens or what vapours may be given off. Commercial names are also inadequate because the manufacturer may change the composition without changing the name.

**commercial name**

**specific name**

Pure substances are given **specific names** by scientists and others who use them frequently. Amongst this group are some simple names such as *toluene*, *thymol* and *borax*. These names refer only to one pure compound and once it has been generally accepted that the name is only ever used to describe this one material with a particular composition and structure, it can be used, without confusion or danger, in giving recipes for conservation treatment or in discussing chemical reactions. However, there is nothing in the names that indicates what the structure or properties might be; they are the chemical equivalent of a person's first name. For this reason they are often called **trivial names**.

**trivial name**

**systematic name**

There is a second group of specific names which have been produced by following agreed rules of naming* and for this reason are called **systematic names**. Examples are *1.1.1. trichloroethane* (Genklene) and *sodium chloride* (common salt). These names contain information about the component parts and in some cases information about the structure of pure substances. Scientists often use a mixture of trivial and systematic names so that they can avoid some of the tongue-twisters that rigid adherence to the rules would produce. This habit results in the loss of some structural information but as long as the name is specific to one substance there is no danger.

## *B* Elements and compounds

If you look at some of these commonly used specific chemical names you will notice that some are single words and some are combinations of these words. For instance, the atmosphere in a city will contain oxygen, nitrogen, argon, carbon dioxide, carbon monoxide, sulphur dioxide and hydrogen sulphide gases. In this example the

---

*For instance the rules devised by the International Union of Pure and Applied Chemistry (IUPAC) in 1957.*

single words name **elements**. The combination names refer to
**compounds**. In the cases given you can see the element names in
the individual parts of the combination, though with slight changes
(sulphur to sulph*ide*, oxygen to ox*ide*). The compound names tell us
which chemical elements have combined to form the chemical compounds. Thus *carbon* and *oxygen* are the names of elements and
*carbon monoxide* and *carbon dioxide* are the names of compounds
formed by different combinations of the two. (The prefixes *mono-*
and *di-* mean one and two, and their use in the names suggest that
carbon dioxide contains twice as much oxygen as carbon monoxide.)

Although there are thousands of distinct compounds these can all
be generated from a relatively small number of different kinds of
particles being stuck together in various combinations. This is the
basis of the **atomic theory** of matter.

Altogether there are about ninety elements occurring naturally on
Earth and another fourteen or so have been made artificially by
nuclear scientists. Each different element is given its own name and
a symbol. The symbol is used for simplicity's sake as a shorthand for
the full name.

In the materials that a conservator is likely to handle, more than
half of the ninety elements will never occur as they are very rare. For
this reason, the names and symbols of fewer than forty elements
need to be learnt. These are listed below. You can see several familiar
names in this list; many of the common elements have been well
known for centuries. Usually the symbol is formed from the first
letter of the name and sometimes one other letter. This second letter
is necessary as there are ninety elements but only twenty-six letters.
Some elements that have been known for a long time have symbols
that are derived from their old Latin names, eg gold (*aurum*).

**element**
**compound**

**atomic theory**

| | | | | | |
|---|---|---|---|---|---|
| aluminium | Al | copper | Cu | oxygen | O |
| antimony | Sb | fluorine | F | phosphorus | P |
| arsenic | As | gold | Au | potassium | K |
| barium | Ba | hydrogen | H | silicon | Si |
| boron | B | iodine | I | silver | Ag |
| bromine | Br | iron | Fe | sodium | Na |
| cadmium | Cd | lead | Pb | sulphur | S |
| calcium | Ca | magnesium | Mg | tin | Sn |
| carbon | C | manganese | Mn | titanium | Ti |
| chlorine | Cl | mercury | Hg | vanadium | V |
| chromium | Cr | nickel | Ni | zinc | Zn |
| cobalt | Co | nitrogen | N | | |

You know from practical experience with charcoal or coke that
carbon is a black solid. You also know that the oxygen you breathe
in and the carbon dioxide you breathe out are colourless transparent
gases. Consequently the compound, carbon dioxide, must be more
than just a finely divided mixture of the black solid and the colourless gas, for the colour and solidity are totally absent in the compound. Similarly, the white metallic lustre of silver is absent in the
black substance formed when it tarnishes. The tarnish is silver sulphide, a compound of the elements silver and sulphur made by

interaction between the metal, silver, and the gas, hydrogen sulphide. The atomic theory of matter explains this by suggesting that all matter is composed of very small particles. All the particles of one element or of one compound are identical but are different from those of any other element or compound. The smallest possible **atom** particle of an element is called an **atom**. In compounds, the *atoms* of elements are joined together in a special arrangement to form a particle that is characteristic of the compound. The particles are **molecule** called **molecules** and the molecules of a single compound are all identical. The links between the atoms in a molecule, which are **bonds** called **bonds**, will be discussed in the following chapters. The symbols for compounds are made up of the individual symbols of the elements of which each is composed (see Chapter 3).

## *C* Atoms and molecules

Molecules may consist of two or more atoms bonded together. Usually the atoms are of several different elements: eg carbon dioxide contains carbon and oxygen atoms; acetone contains carbon, hydrogen and oxygen atoms; chloroform contains carbon, hydrogen and chlorine atoms. It is very unusual for a molecule to contain more than seven elements; two, three or four is the common range. Gaseous elements like oxygen, nitrogen and chlorine are not found as single atoms but as molecules containing two atoms of the same element. The atoms of solid elements are joined in much larger groups. An atom with no bond to another atom is very rare; it only occurs in the unreactive gases like argon and in the vapours of metals.

Although there is only a limited number of different atoms that can combine to form compounds, and less than forty elements commonly occur, the number of possible combinations is very great, especially when you consider that large numbers of several different atoms can be linked together to form a molecule. We shall see that the properties of this vast range of compounds are as much determined by the nature of the bonding between atoms as by the number and type of atoms themselves.

## *D* Solids, liquids and gases

The fact that substances can exist as solids, liquids or gases, and can change from one of these states to another, is explained by a further extension of the atomic theory. For example, water is a compound which is liquid at ordinary temperatures, freezes at 0°C becoming a solid, and boils at 100°C to become a gas. If you heat ice above 0°C it turns back to liquid and, similarly, by cooling the gas (steam) to below 100°C that too will turn back to a liquid, a fact used in purifying water by distillation.

The atomic theory's description of this is that molecules are firmly and closely stuck together in a solid, only loosely held in liquids, and quite free from each other in gases. Already you will realise that some important properties are being explained. The rigidity of solids is accounted for by forces holding the particles together. The observation that many solids occur as regular geometric crystals is consistent with the idea of large numbers of identical particles. Regular stacking of many uniform shapes, like cans in a supermarket display, results in pyramids with edges, faces and points like those found in crystals.

The reason that liquids can flow is because these **inter-molecular forces** (that is, the forces *between* separate molecules) are not so strong. That is why you can stir or pour liquids. High divers plunge into water with the confident expectation that the molecules will move out of their way, while in winter conditions of 0°C or below the same water becomes capable of carrying the weight of skaters because the molecules are held tightly together as ice.

**inter-molecular forces**

In *gases*, mobility is even easier because the molecules are completely separated. A kilogram of water about to boil occupies just over one litre of space. As steam at 100°C the same molecules can separate to reach all parts of the room.

Although the atomic concept can explain the existence of the three physical states (solid, liquid and gas) it has given no intimation of the role of heat in the transition from one condition to another. The hotter things are, the faster the particles move.

In gases atoms and molecules move about rapidly, colliding frequently, and there is a great deal of empty space between them. They move more slowly in liquids and slower still in solids where they are packed tightly together, with just a little freedom to vibrate to and fro. If the solid is made hotter, its molecules will move more rapidly. The faster they move, the more space they need to move in and so the substance expands and eventually passes from solid to liquid, and then, from liquid to vapour. The temperature at which the transition between solid and liquid occurs is the **melting or freezing point** and between liquid and vapour, the **boiling point**.

**melting or freezing and boiling points**

The observation that the smells of substances such as resins and solvents spread rapidly throughout the room from someone's workbench, suggests that the molecules of volatile substances are able to travel rapidly in the atmosphere in the form of vapours.

As a demonstration of this fill a beaker with water. Then take a crystal of a deeply coloured water-soluble substance such as potassium permanganate and drop it into the water. Do not stir the water. Even without stirring, the liquid gradually changes colour throughout. The only explanation of this is that the particles are in **random motion** and that it is this random movement of particles which has produced an evenly mixed solution.

**random motion**

# *E* Mixtures and purity

It has already been noted that there is a remarkable difference between a *mixture* of two separate elements and a *compound* of the same two elements. In a mixture the elements retain their individual properties rather than assuming the properties of the compound they might form. In a compound there are strong bonds between the constituent atoms. In a mixture, however, there are no chemical bonds between the components.

Generally speaking all materials whether synthetic or naturally occurring are *mixtures* of several kinds of molecules or atoms but, in mixing, these different particles have not undergone any chemical interaction or change. Different mixtures exist at many levels of **intimacy**. A house is a mixture of bricks, mortar, plaster, wood, nails, etc., though it seems perverse to regard it this way because the bits are quite distinct. Concrete, which is a mixture of cement, sand and gravel, is a more realistic example of a mixture, perhaps, because the separate components are purposely mixed together to make it. An understanding of these rather obvious, coarse mixtures is important to conservators. Often, in the course of your work, you will be confronted by an object composed of a variety of materials and you will be prevented from using a technique because the beneficial effects on one part of it will be outweighed by adverse effects on another. A very strong solvent, for example, might have the unwanted effect of softening the paint layer as well as removing a discoloured varnish from a painting.

It is worth noting that much of your work, all cleaning for instance, involves separating mixtures – the artefact and the dirt – and you will know very well that the difficulty of these jobs depends, to some extent, on how intimately mixed the two parts are.

**intimate mixture**

**Figure 2.1** *Cast iron, under the microscope. The dark lines are carbon, in an iron matrix.*

**Figure 2.2** *Electron microscope picture of Roman Samian ware, showing that it is a mixture of different materials.*

The most intimate mixtures are those at the level of atoms or molecules. Gases mix easily at the molecular level. The Earth's atmosphere is a good example of an intimate mixture of several kinds of atoms and molecules. Since air is 80% nitrogen you *might* call it impure nitrogen but that would miss most of its important properties. As a source of oxygen, water and carbon dioxide it is essential to life, and you would not face so many conservation problems if the sulphur compounds were absent. (Hydrogen sulphide is the agent which tarnishes silver, and sulphur dioxide causes the degradation of masonry and other materials.)

**Solutions** form another common class of molecularly intimate **solutions** mixtures. There are many familiar examples of substances dissolved in water – sugar in tea, salt in the sea, dilute acids and alkalis used in your workshop. Among the mixtures you make yourself during your work are those achieved by adding wetting agents (detergents, etc.) to water, mixing two-component glues like Araldite (here the ingredients *are* chemically interactive) and adding pigments to adhesives and fillers (see Book III). It is rare to find a substance that contains only one kind of atom or molecule. The most likely place you might expect to find matter containing only one kind of molecule is among the jars and bottles of chemicals you keep in your workshop. Most of these will be examples of compounds. If it were possible to have a specimen with only one kind of molecule present it would be referred to as a *pure compound*.

There will, however, invariably be some molecules of other compounds present, and these are called impurities. You may have a chemical in your workshop with a label bearing the word "Analar". This is a quality rating; the label will inform you what percentages of which impurities are present. A price list of chemicals from one of the suppliers will usually list the following categories:

**purity**

"Spectrographic grade" or "Spec-Pure"    — very, very pure
"Analar"                                                        — very pure
"Commercial grade" or "Industrial grade" — fairly pure.

Industrial grade is usually quite adequate for conservation purposes unless it is known that an unwanted reaction with one of the impurities can occur. With organic solvents such as acetone there is occasionally an undesirable residue after evaporation. Spectrographic grade is only needed in chemical analysis where it is important that no stray compounds interfere with the detection and measurement of very small quantities of material. Generally, because of the effort involved in removing the last traces of impurities, you will pay a lot more for a very nearly pure chemical than one where there is a higher proportion of impurities. Compare the price of supermarket washing soda with that of "Analar" sodium carbonate.

# *F* Physical and chemical changes

Changes in the condition of materials are always important to the conservator. The deterioration of objects to a state where they need active conservation treatment is the result of change. You work to arrest those changes, at least, and sometimes to reverse them. The

**physical changes**
**chemical changes**

changes during both deterioration and conservation treatment can be classified as either **physical changes** or **chemical changes**.

A *physical* change of condition involves a rearrangement of the molecules without any change in the structure of the individual molecules. *Chemical* changes involve rearrangements of atoms among molecules to create new molecular structures.

The components of a mixture can be separated by a physical change, whereas when the atoms in a molecule are permanently separated a chemical change has taken place.

A great deal of conservation treatment uses physical changes. If you blow the dust off a museum exhibit you have merely moved the dust from one place to another, you haven't wrought any chemical changes upon its molecules. Similarly when wax is used as a thermoplastic adhesive (for example, in attaching a lining canvas onto the back of an original canvas) it is melted by heat and flows into the two canvases. When it cools the molecules of wax cease to move and begin to hold the canvases together. This is a physical change. Another physical change occurs when a spirit varnish, like a solution of Ketone-N in white spirit, dries on a surface. The solvent, white spirit, evaporates, leaving a film of resin behind. The solvent molecules have left the surface and the resin molecules have remained; there has been no rearrangement *within* the molecules.

The tarnishing of silver, however, is a chemical change. Silver atoms combine with sulphur atoms to form black silver sulphide. The corrosion of bronze and the rusting of iron are also chemical changes.

It is not always easy to differentiate between physical and chemical changes. Cleaning processes involving solvents or washing with detergents are examples where the distinction between physical and chemical changes is more blurred since both may be involved. (Consideration of these processes will be left until Book II.)

# G How chemical reactions happen

During the course of this chapter you will have come to think of the molecules of a compound as atoms bonded together into characteristic patterns. Chemical change has been explained as a rearrangement of atoms among molecules. To understand how these changes can happen you need to know what causes the atoms to break their bonds to form new patterns.

When a substance is heated the atoms and molecules move with increasing speed, and so, you can imagine, they run increasing risks of colliding, and with greater impact. As they collide with one another the particles may join together or knock parts off each other. These fragments may recombine to form new combinations of atoms. The more stable (strongly formed) a molecule is, the stronger the forces that are needed to break it up and cause it to react chemically, that is to make new combinations. This image of particles in constant movement, with the movement increasing with the increase of temperature, explains why chemical reactions tend to go faster at higher temperatures. As the collision speeds of particles get higher molecules may start to break at more points in their structure, creating a greater variety of pieces free to combine and form a range of fresh molecules. It is also likely that while parts of molecules are randomly moving and colliding together they may temporarily bond to form an unstable mass which easily falls apart to form yet other molecules which may be more stable (firmly bonded together).

**Figure 2.3**  *One possible way in which molecules may collide, join, and then break up during a reaction.*

As a conservator, you will quickly understand from this that there are good reasons why, if the instructions for a chemical treatment of an object specify a temperature, you should keep to it. Otherwise the proposed reaction may go too fast to allow control or reactions different from those intended may occur.

# Molecules and chemical equations

*A*   Visualising molecules

*B*   Symbolic representations of molecules

  *B1*   *Molecular formulae*
  *B2*   *Structural formulae*

*C*   Building chemical equations

*D*   Chemical equations in use

  *D1*   *The manufacture and deterioration of fresco wall paintings*
  *D2*   *The deterioration and subsequent treatment of lead white pigment*

*E*   Making chemistry quantative

  *E1*   *Atomic and molecular quantities*
  *E2*   *Molar quantities*
  *E3*   *Molar solutions*

# Molecules and chemical equations

## *A* Visualising molecules

Most people find it easier to understand something if they can hold some sort of visual image in their minds. Individual molecules are too small to be seen, even with powerful microscopes. The smallest thing you can see through a good optical microscope is about ten thousand atoms in diameter. This makes it unrealistic to ask what molecules look like or what colour they are. Nevertheless, they do have a three-dimensional reality which must be related to what we call the ''shape'' of visible objects.

The individual atoms of which molecules are composed can be thought of as elastic spheres, but in molecules the distance between the centres of these spheres is so small that the atomic shapes must be merged into each other. A realistic way to show the shape of a molecule, for example of oxygen, is this:

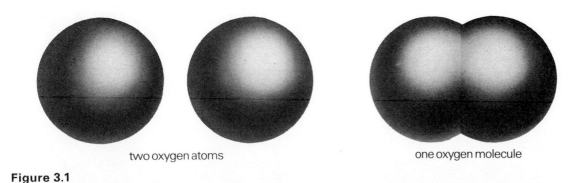

two oxygen atoms                    one oxygen molecule

**Figure 3.1**

Known facts about the behaviour of gases are consistent with this picture of molecules, and suggest that they do have shape and volume, but being squashy, do not have rigid outlines.

Methane, formerly called marsh gas and now known as natural gas, has molecules that contain four hydrogen atoms and one carbon atom. It is known that none of the four hydrogen atoms is joined to another but that each is bonded individually to a central carbon atom. The hydrogen atoms surround the carbon atom, keeping as far away from each other as possible. This means that the hydrogen atoms are at the corners of a triangular pyramid (tetrahedron) with the carbon atom in the middle.

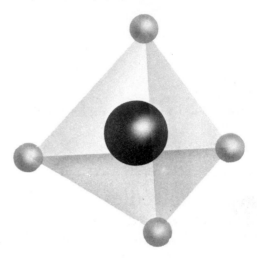

**Figure 3.2**  *Schematic representation of methane molecule.*

**molecular models**

Figure 3.2 immediately shows the difficulty of representing this knowledge on flat paper even for so simple a molecule. The most realistic way to portray three-dimensional reality is to use three-dimensional models. These are often used for teaching science and are of two types.

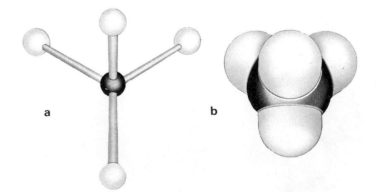

a          b

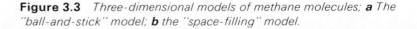

**Figure 3.3**  *Three-dimensional models of methane molecules;* **a** *The "ball-and-stick" model;* **b** *the "space-filling" model.*

Ball and stick models show the links (bonds) between atoms clearly, but obscure the fact that in reality the atoms merge together, as the space-filling models show. Although both types of model provide useful information they may also suggest things that are probably not true of the actual molecules. For instance, in both types of model the atoms of different elements are shown in different colours and there is an obvious division between the different atoms. The models are designed to come apart to show how molecules can decompose and rearrange, but the links are always rigid, which obscures the fact that bonds in molecules are very stretchy.

# *B* Symbolic representations of molecules

Owing to the practical difficulties of depicting molecules accurately, more symbolic ways of representing them are used by scientists. These are much more useful than the ones we have just seen for discussing chemical reactions. Consequently they are the ones most frequently found in chemistry books and in conservation texts.

## B1 Molecular formulae

The first of these more symbolic models is the **molecular formula**. It tells concisely how many atoms of which elements are contained in each molecule of a compound.

**molecular formula**

The molecular formula for methane is $CH_4$. Comparing this combination of two letters and a number with the pictures in figures 3.2 and 3.3 shows you immediately that it describes the molecule as having one carbon atom and four hydrogen atoms. The elements present are identified by their symbols (see page 33 in Chapter 2), and there is another convention to show how many of each sort of atom is present. Although the information might have been written CHHHH, the convention is to represent any number of atoms greater than one by a little numeral at the bottom right-hand corner of the element's symbol (a **subscript**). Thus in $CH_4$ the letter C stands for *one* atom of carbon and $H_4$ for *four* atoms of hydrogen. (The symbols must always be written carefully; Co is the symbol for cobalt but CO is the molecular formula for carbon monoxide.)

**subscript**

*Exercises*

In order to help you become familiar with writing molecular formulae it may be useful for you to do the following:

1 Write in the appropriate numbers in the blank spaces in the following examples;

    **a** the molecular formula for carbon dioxide is $CO_2$. Each molecule contains _____ atom(s) of carbon and _____ atom(s) of oxygen.

    **b** the molecular formula for sulphuric acid is $H_2SO_4$. Each molecule contains _____ atom(s) of hydrogen, _____ atom(s) of sulphur and _____ atom(s) of oxygen.

c the molecular formula of acetone is $C_3H_6O$. Each molecule contains ———— atom(s) of carbon, ———— atom(s) of hydrogen and ———— atom(s) of oxygen.

2 Write down molecular formulae for the following molecules:

a water, which contains two atoms of hydrogen and one atom of oxygen.
b ammonia, which contains one atom of nitrogen and three atoms of hydrogen.
c benzene, which contains six atoms of carbon and six atoms of hydrogen.

## B2 Structural formulae

Molecular formulae only give limited information, however, and do not, for instance, tell us which atoms are joined to which. This information is conveyed in another representation – the **structural formula**. The structural formula for methane is:

**structural formula**

$$
\begin{array}{c}
\text{H} \\
| \\
\text{H}-\text{C}-\text{H} \\
| \\
\text{H}
\end{array}
$$

where each atom is represented by its symbol and the bonds between them are shown as dashes. Although this shows which atom is joined to which, it is still a flat representation of what, in reality is a three-dimensional entity. Consequently, you will sometimes see attempts to present a more three-dimensional view within structural formulae, such as Figure 3.4.

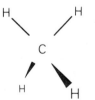

**Figure 3.4** *Another representation of methane, which uses a form of perspective to suggest the molecule's three-dimensional shape.*

With large, more complicated molecules, their shape actually dictates how they react and so a two-dimensional representation of a three-dimensional shape is often necessary.

### Structural formulae and isomers

The molecular formula for ethyl alcohol (the major constituent of methylated spirits) is $C_2H_6O$. Figure 3.5(a) shows its structural formula, while Figure 3.5(b), although composed of the same numbers of carbon, hydrogen and oxygen atoms, is not the structural formula for ethyl alcohol. When the atoms are linked together in this way the compound is called dimethyl ether.

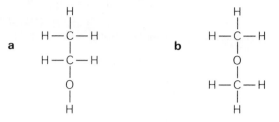

**Figure 3.5**  *Structural formulae for $C_2H_6O$.*

There are many groups of compounds that have the same molecular formula but have different structures. Such compounds are called **isomers**.

**isomers**

There are three possible isomers of $C_2H_4O$. One is called ethylene oxide (Figure 3.6a) and another is acetaldehyde (Figure 3.6b).

**Figure 3.6**  *Structures for $C_2H_4O$.*

Ethylene oxide is a gas used to eradicate wood-boring insects. When it is heated, ethylene oxide is converted into its isomer acetaldehyde.

Two new features are shown in Figure 3.6. In ethylene oxide the atoms are joined together in a ring, which is quite a common structure. In the formula for acetaldehyde there is a double dash between the C and the O. This means that the bond between C and O in this molecule is not the same as the C — O bonds in ethyl alcohol, ethylene oxide or dimethyl ether. The different kinds of links between atoms will be explained more fully in the next chapter. The point which it is important for you to understand now is that molecules which have the same molecular formula can show quite different chemical properties *because they have different structures*. With experience you will come to anticipate some of the properties of a particular molecule by looking at its structural formula.

The fact that chemical behaviour depends on *structure* as well as what atoms a molecule contains, leads to the further development of molecular formulae to indicate more about molecular structure. The molecular formula for ethyl alcohol can be written as $C_2H_5OH$, that of dimethyl ether as $CH_3OCH_3$ and that of acetaldehyde as $CH_3CHO$. These compact representations give almost as much information as full structure diagrams. Unfortunately ring compounds such as ethylene oxide cannot be easily represented by a string of symbols.

# C Building chemical equations

In the preceding section you have seen representations of oxygen and methane molecules. Both are gases at ordinary temperatures,

**chemical reaction**

oxygen being a constituent of the air, and methane being the gas pumped through the gas mains as a fuel. When a gas burner is lit a **chemical reaction** is started between these two gases. Beyond the edge of the flame you would be unlikely to find any methane molecules. Instead, there are two different gases, water (as a gas because of the heat of the flame) and carbon dioxide. The *reaction* is the process by which methane and oxygen become carbon dioxide and water.

This could be written down in words:

Methane *mixed with* oxygen *and ignited*
*turns into* carbon dioxide *mixed with* water.

Obviously such descriptions rapidly become cumbersome while imparting only limited information, and so symbols are used instead. "Mixed with" can be denoted simply by $+$, "turns into" by $\rightarrow$. Special instructions like "ignited", in this case a description of the necessary temperature to effect a reaction (say 500°C), are written on the arrow.

$$\text{Methane} + \text{oxygen} \xrightarrow{500°C} \text{carbon dioxide} + \text{water}$$

The next step is to use molecular formulae for the substances. Carbon dioxide is $CO_2$ (one atom of carbon and two of oxygen), water is $H_2O$ (two atoms of hydrogen with one of oxygen) and so what *might* be written is this:

$$CH_4 + O_2 \xrightarrow{500°C} CO_2 + H_2O$$

**reactants**
**products**


**equation**

In this form, the description of the reaction starts to become useful for understanding more about what is happening. For example, if the chemicals were weighed before and after the reaction, assuming no part of any substance had been lost, you would find no change in weight. The weight of the **reactants** (the chemicals you start with) is equal to the weight of the **products** (what you finish with). This is because *no atoms are destroyed or made during the reaction*; the event is just a *rearrangement of the atoms* you first had. The **equation** (as this symbolic description of a reaction is called) should show that the number of oxygen atoms is unchanged and so is the number of hydrogen atoms, although all the atoms are combined differently with one another. Look at it again:

$$CH_4 + O_2 \xrightarrow{500°C} CO_2 + H_2O$$

$$\text{methane} + \text{oxygen} \xrightarrow{500°C} \text{carbon dioxide} + \text{water}$$

**balancing**

Think of the formulae not as mere shorthand for the names, but as representing *one molecule* of each chemical. You will then see that the four hydrogen atoms at the start appear to have turned into just two and that the two oxygen atoms have increased to three at the right hand side of the equation. In order to **balance** the equation and maintain the same number of atoms on each side, it is necessary, therefore, to find the number of molecules which react together to change methane and oxygen into carbon dioxide and water without any implied destruction or creation of atoms. Try this:

$$CH_4 \quad + \quad \underline{2}O_2 \quad \rightarrow \quad CO_2 \quad + \quad \underline{2}H_2O$$

| one molecule of methane | + | two molecules of oxygen | → | one molecule of carbon dioxide | + | two molecules of water |

The 2s are saying that there are *two* molecules of $O_2$ and *two* molecules of $H_2O$ involved.

Now count the atoms of each kind on each side of the reaction:

**Atoms present**

| Element | Before | After |
|---------|--------|-------|
| C | 1 | 1 |
| H | 4 | $2 \times 2 = 4$ |
| O | $2 \times 2 = 4$ | $2 + (2 \times 1) = 4$ |

This complete description tells you how many molecules of different sorts react together. It is called a **balanced chemical equation** once the number of each type of atom is the same on either side of the arrow. Balanced equations used to be shown with an equals sign instead of the arrow which is why we have the word "equation". Whenever a chemical reaction is represented by a chemical equation it should be balanced, because otherwise it does not convey all the information it can. As the next section will reveal, balanced equations allow an interpretation of events on the minute scale of atoms and molecules. The ability to understand these descriptions of chemical reactions will often be of great value to you in your work.

**balanced chemical equation**

*Exercise*

3  Try balancing the equations for the reactions in which propane ($C_3H_8$) and butane ($C_4H_{10}$) are burned in oxygen to form carbon dioxide and water.

# D  Chemical equations in use

Chemistry can help you understand more thoroughly the nature of the changes which occur when an object is manufactured, as it ages and deteriorates, and when it is treated. It can suggest why objects made of particular materials are subject to particular forms of change; you can use this knowledge to reduce or prevent further damage and to judge the suitability of conservation treatments.

This section gives two examples to show how your knowledge gained through observation can be illuminated further by knowing some chemistry.

### D1 The manufacture and deterioration of fresco wall paintings

Listed below are the chemical names and molecular formulae for all the materials which are introduced in this section. Although you may find these a little foreign to you at present, much more will be said about how these formulae are arrived at and what the names mean, in Chapters 4 and 5 respectively. This need not worry you at present, although it may help you to refer to the table given in Chapter 2 on page 33 so that you can remind yourself of the short-hand symbols for the various elements listed. The last four sub-

**crystals**

stances in the list are solid **crystals** in their normal states. You will learn later that it is more accurate to think of them as having an extended structure, rather than consisting of individual molecules; but their molecular formulae can be used in chemical equations in exactly the same way as simple molecules like methane and oxygen.

| Chemical name | Material | Molecular formula |
| --- | --- | --- |
| water | water | $H_2O$ |
| sulphur dioxide | | $SO_2$ |
| sulphur trioxide | | $SO_3$ |
| sulphuric acid | | $H_2SO_4$ |
| carbon dioxide | | $CO_2$ |
| silicon dioxide | sand, silica | $SiO_2$ |
| calcium oxide | lime, quicklime | $CaO$ |
| calcium carbonate | chalk, limestone | $CaCO_3$ |
| calcium sulphate | | $CaSO_4$ |
| calcium hydroxide | slaked lime | $Ca(OH)_2$ |

The bracket $(OH)_2$ indicates that there are two of the OH group.

In *Il Libro dell'Arte (The Craftsman's Handbook)* by Cennino D'Andrea Cennini,* "The Method and System for Working on a Wall, that is, in Fresco", the preparation of the wall (application of the *arricio*) is described as follows:

"When you want to work on a wall, which is the most agreeable and impressive kind of work, first of all get some lime and some sand, each of them well sifted ... and wet them up well with water, and wet up enough to last you two or three weeks. And let it stand for a day or so, until the heat goes out of it: for when it is so hot, the plaster which you put on cracks afterward. When you are ready to plaster, first sweep the wall well, and wet it down thoroughly, for you cannot get it too wet. And take your lime mortar, well worked over, a trowelful at a time; and plaster once or twice, to begin with, to get this plaster flat on the wall. Then, when you want to work, remember first to make this plaster quite uneven and fairly rough."

When the *arricio* had dried (after some days) a second layer of plaster (*intonaco*) was applied on the morning of the day on which the painting was to be done; the area that was covered was limited to the amount that the artist thought that he could complete in a day's work. The artist then painted pigments mixed with water over the fresh plaster.

If you look at the list given at the beginning of this section, the raw materials for the plaster (lime, sand and water) are the chemicals

---

*"Il Libro Dell'Arte" translated by D.V. Thompson, New York (1960).

calcium oxide, silica and water; and yet when a piece of antique fresco is analysed the chemicals found are silica and calcium carbonate. Clearly some rearrangements of atoms among molecules (chemical reactions) have taken place.

Here are the equations describing the chemical reactions which occur:

$$CaO + H_2O \rightarrow Ca(OH)_2$$

$$Ca(OH)_2 + CO_2 \rightarrow CaCO_3 + H_2O$$

Before you read on, look again at Cennini's account, and at the list of molecular formulae. Using the information in these and your knowledge of chemical reactions see whether you can:

1 Say what these two reactions are in words.
2 Deduce when the first reaction takes place.
3 Say where the carbon dioxide involved in the second reaction might come from.
4 Decide whether sand is involved in the reactions.
5 Say where the water has gone.

The first reaction to occur takes place when the sand ($SiO_2$) and lime ($CaO$) are mixed with water and slaked lime ($Ca(OH)_2$) is formed. More water than is necessary for the reaction is used so that the plaster is a workable paste. Looking at the equations above, the formula $SiO_2$ does not appear. This implies that the sand constituent of plaster does not take part in either of the chemical reactions; it is only there to help strengthen the plaster. The second reaction describes one "molecule" of calcium hydroxide reacting with one molecule of carbon dioxide and producing one "molecule" of calcium carbonate and one of water. The carbon dioxide involved in this reaction comes from the air and the reaction takes place over a period of months as air diffuses into the plaster. It may even take years for the hydroxide to be converted into carbonate through the whole thickness of the *arricio*. Spare water gradually evaporates from the wall as the plaster dries out. It is probably the spaces left by the water which provide porosity in the plaster through which air can penetrate to produce the second reaction.

There are many frescoes (especially, for example, in Venice) made in the way described, and which have suffered serious deterioration in the industrially polluted atmosphere of the city. The main pollutant is sulphur dioxide generated by burning the small quantity of sulphur present naturally in fossil fuels (coal, oil and natural gas).

In a polluted atmosphere two reactions take place. Refer back to the list on page 50 to determine what the names of the reactants and products of the two reactions are:

$$SO_2 + O_2 \rightarrow SO_3$$

$$SO_3 + H_2O \rightarrow H_2SO_4$$

However, one of these equations is not *balanced*. Can you deduce which of the equations it is and how it can be made to balance?

The first equation has one more oxygen atom on the left-hand side than on the right. To make it balance *two* molecules of sulphur dioxide need to combine with one molecule of oxygen forming two molecules of sulphur trioxide as the product of the reaction.

### Demonstration

Take a chip (about one cm³) of marble, limestone or chalk (not blackboard "chalk":), which are all calcium carbonate, and some dilute sulphuric acid. (Handle acids with care.) Try putting the chip in the acid and leaving it there for a few hours. What evidence of chemical reaction is there to be seen?

The reaction between calcium carbonate and sulphuric acid is described by the equation:

$$CaCO_3 + H_2SO_4 \rightarrow CaSO_4 + H_2O + CO_2$$

Observing this demonstration, you will have seen bubbles of gas rising from the chip and eventually found that the chip has dissolved in the acid. The reaction is one way of helping to identify calcium carbonate. The demonstration also shows you in action how the decay of frescoes, marble statuary and lime mortar in brickwork can be accelerated in the presence of sulphuric acid. Clearly the best long term preventive measure would be to take steps to reduce the emission of sulphur dioxide into the air. However, the problems that face the conservator are immediate. Knowing the chemistry of the problem tells you that the object must be kept dry and that polluted air should be excluded from it if further deterioration is to be prevented.

## D2 The deterioration and subsequent treatment of lead white pigment

All the following compounds appear in this example and are listed here as a guide when reading the related text.

| Chemical Name | Material | Molecular formula |
|---|---|---|
| water | | $H_2O$ |
| hydrogen peroxide | peroxide | $H_2O_2$ |
| carbon dioxide | | $CO_2$ |
| hydrogen sulphide | | $H_2S$ |
| lead carbonate | | $PbCO_3$ |
| basic lead carbonate | lead white | $Pb_2CO_3(OH)_2$ |
| lead hydroxide | | $Pb(OH)_2$ |
| lead sulphide | | $PbS$ |
| lead sulphate | | $PbSO_4$ |

Lead white, as you can see from the list, is in reality a single compound ($Pb_2CO_3(OH)_2$), although it can be considered as reacting as two distinct compounds ($Pb(OH)_2$ and $PbCO_3$). It is therefore, sometimes written as the two compounds joined by a dot: $PbCO_3 . Pb(OH)_2$

Lead white is not an uncommon pigment. Unfortunately it may turn to black lead sulphide in an atmosphere polluted with hydrogen sulphide gas. Hydrogen sulphide is always present in traces in the air. It is released during the decomposition of plants and animals; it is the gas with the characteristic smell of rotten eggs.

The equation for the reaction between lead carbonate and hydrogen sulphide to produce lead sulphide is:

$$PbCO_3 + H_2S \rightarrow PbS + CO_2 + H_2O$$

The equation for the reaction between lead hydroxide and hydrogen sulphide is:

$$Pb(OH)_2 + H_2S \rightarrow PbS + 2H_2O$$

Adding these two descriptions together gives the equation for lead white reacting with hydrogen sulphide:

$$PbCO_3.Pb(OH)_2 + 2H_2S \rightarrow 2PbS + CO_2 + 3H_2O$$

In conservation, watercolours, pastels and miniatures disfigured by their lead white having turned black are often treated with hydrogen peroxide. Hydrogen peroxide ($H_2O_2$) is a very unstable compound and its molecules easily fall apart releasing oxygen and water. You have probably used ''peroxide'' as a gentle bleach on organic stains – it is effective because the freed oxygen reacts with the molecules which produce the colour. Its action on lead sulphide is to convert this black matter to lead sulphate which is white, although *not* the original pigment.

$$PbS + 4H_2O_2 \rightarrow PbSO_4 + 4H_2O$$

The two examples just discussed show how the conservator is helped by chemical insight into the causes of deterioration. The ability to understand chemical equations has offered precise and concise descriptions of what is occurring.

---

*Exercises*

4  Lime is prepared from limestone or chalk which is heated in a lime kiln. The heat decomposes the calcium carbonate (of which both chalk and limestone are composed) into calcium oxide (lime) and carbon dioxide gas is given off. The kiln is usually heated by a coke burning oven. The lime sinks to the bottom of the kiln and is removed.

   Write down the chemical equation for this reaction.

5  Suggest a possible reaction between calcium carbonate and sulphuric acid. Calcium sulphate is one of the products. Write the chemical equation.

6  This reaction between calcium carbonate and sulphuric acid may be used to distinguish between calcium carbonate and calcium sulphate. There is no reaction between sulphuric acid and calcium sulphate. The reaction might be used to determine whether the material in the ground of a painting is chalk or gesso, that is, whether it is calcium carbonate or sulphate. A small sample of

the material in question is placed on a microscope slide and a drop of dilute sulphuric acid ($H_2SO_4$) is added. If the material being treated is calcium carbonate then bubbles can be seen rising from the sample floating in the acid. No such bubbles are visible if the sample is calcium sulphate.

What are these bubbles?

# *E* Making chemistry quantitative

## E1 Atomic and molecular quantities

quantities

A molecular formula tells you what a material is made of, but when this knowledge is applied to a conservation problem it is often necessary to know the **quantities** of the materials involved in the treatment. You may, for example, want to know how much of one substance will react with a certain amount of another. Realistic quantities of the materials you handle can be measured by weighing in the normal way. Balanced equations, on the other hand, refer to small numbers of molecules. They describe the reactions of such *minute* quantities of substances that it is impossible to employ the usual practical procedures for measuring. To derive weights of materials from balanced equations requires the reasonable supposition, the basis of atomic theory, that atoms are permanent and that all atoms of the same element weigh the same. You could not make measurements to calculate how much lime would be produced from a given amount of chalk just using one molecule of calcium carbonate. There would have to be a measurable quantity of carbonate. The amount of lime produced would be a definite percentage of the amount of chalk from which it was made. The equation for the whole lump of chalk being converted to lime would be:

$$nCaCO_3 \xrightarrow{\text{heat}} nCaO \quad + \quad nCO_2$$

| n molecules of | n molecules of | n molecules of |
| calcium carbonate | + | calcium oxide | + | carbon dioxide |

where n is used to represent some enormous number.

### *Atomic and molecular masses*

mass
weight

Before we can get any further with this problem you must learn something about the weights of individual atoms. Before we can do this you must understand that there is a slight difference between the terms weight and mass. **Mass** is a measure of the amount of matter and is a universally constant property of matter. **Weight** is the force that pulls the matter downwards and is dependant on the local gravitational field. So a given mass will have different weights on the moon, in Mexico City or in London. Although the words *mass* and *weight* are often used interchangeably it is more correct to refer to atomic and molecular *mass* rather than atomic weight and molecular weight.

In the early days of modern chemistry it was a problem to make consistent measurements of the masses of atoms and molecules, although nowadays, there are instruments (**mass-spectrometers**) which can determine the mass of single atoms and molecules. There is now a very accurate scale of the masses of the different elements' atoms relative to one another. This is known as the scale of **relative atomic masses** although it is often (and less precisely) referred to as the scale of atomic weights. For your practical purposes, however, the minute accuracy available from modern techniques is not often needed, and a simple scale of relative atomic masses will be used in this book. This gives a hydrogen atom, the lightest of all atoms, a mass of one unit. The atomic masses of the other elements are expressed as multiples of this mass. A list of atomic masses for the more common elements is shown below. The figures are given to the nearest whole number, but the margin of error in doing this is usually less than one percent.

**mass-spectrometers**

**relative atomic mass**

**hydrogen atom mass**

| Element | Chemical symbol | Atomic mass | Element | Chemical symbol | Atomic mass |
|---------|-----------------|-------------|---------|-----------------|-------------|
| aluminium | Al | 27 | lead | Pb | 207 |
| antimony | Sb | 122 | magnesium | Mg | 24 |
| arsenic | As | 75 | manganese | Mn | 55 |
| barium | Ba | 137 | mercury | Hg | 201 |
| boron | B | 11 | nickel | Ni | 59 |
| bromine | Br | 80 | nitrogen | N | 14 |
| cadmium | Cd | 112 | oxygen | O | 16 |
| calcium | Ca | 40 | phosphorus | P | 31 |
| carbon | C | 12 | potassium | K | 39 |
| chlorine | Cl | 35 | silicon | Si | 28 |
| chromium | Cr | 52 | silver | Ag | 108 |
| cobalt | Co | 59 | sodium | Na | 23 |
| copper | Cu | 64 | sulphur | S | 32 |
| fluorine | F | 19 | tin | Sn | 119 |
| gold | Au | 197 | titanium | Ti | 48 |
| hydrogen | H | 1 | vanadium | V | 51 |
| iodine | I | 127 | zinc | Zn | 65 |
| iron | Fe | 56 | | | |

**Figure 3.7** *Approximate atomic masses of the commoner elements.*

With this set of atomic masses and the knowledge you have already acquired of molecular formulae, you will be able to work out how heavy one molecule is compared with another. These **relative molecular masses** (familiarly, but not so correctly, called molecular weights) are found by adding together the atomic masses of all the atoms contained in each molecule, using the molecular formula to tell you how many times the atomic mass of each element has to be added in. Going back to the lime-burning equation, for example:

**relative molecular masses**

$$CaCO_3 \xrightarrow{\text{heat}} CaO + CO_2$$

The molecular mass of calcium carbonate ($CaCO_3$), can be calculated by adding together the atomic masses of *one* atom of calcium, *one* atom of carbon and *three* atoms of oxygen (because there are three oxygen atoms in the formula). The total is the molecular mass of calcium carbonate.

Thus:  1 × Ca atomic mass                              = 40
       + 1 × C      ,,      ,,                          = 12
       + 3 × O      ,,      masses at 16 each           = 48

Molecular mass of $CaCO_3$                             = 100

Similarly, for quicklime (CaO) and carbon dioxide ($CO_2$) the simple sums can be laid out:

    1 × atomic mass of Ca at 40      = 40
    + 1 × atomic mass of O  at 16    = 16

Molecular mass of CaO                = 56

    1 × atomic mass of C at 12         = 12
    + 2 × atomic mass of O at 16 each  = 32

Molecular mass of $CO_2$               = 44

You can now see the logic of the argument. The yield of lime from limestone is 56% because each "molecule" of calcium oxide weighs 56/100 of the calcium carbonate "molecule" from which it comes.

*Exercise*

8 Using the same process and consulting Figure 3.7 work out molecular masses for (a) methane, (b) oxygen *molecules* and (c) water.

## E2 Molar quantities

Look again at the balanced equation for the combustion of methane (page 48) and then at the relative masses of the molecules written here below the formulae:

$$CH_4 + 2O_2 \rightarrow CO_2 + 2H_2O$$

$$16 + 2 \times 32 \rightarrow 44 + 2 \times 18$$

$$16 + 64 \rightarrow 44 + 36$$

$$80 \rightarrow 80$$

The units of mass used are, as you will remember, hydrogen atom masses. Hydrogen atom masses are, however, inconveniently small units to measure sensible amounts of materials, and in practice grams, or pounds, or tons can be more suitable, depending on the context. Using hydrogen atom units you can see that the mass of oxygen reacting (64) is related to the mass of methane (16) by a ratio of four to one ($64 : 16 = 4 : 1$). In other words, the oxygen mass equals four times the methane mass. Because this is a measurement of proportion it doesn't matter *what* units are used to measure their relationship. Four times as much oxygen as methane by mass might need to be measured in tons if a gas main fractured and caught fire. Certainly the quantities involved then would be more than one molecule of methane and two of oxygen. The *proportion* would remain the same, that is, for *every* one molecule of methane two of oxygen are used. For every ton of methane burned, four tons of oxygen would be needed.

Because the mass of every methane molecule is the same and remains constant, one gram of methane will always contain the same number of molecules. From the equation we can see that twice that number of molecules of oxygen are used, and will have four times that mass, 4g. Put another way, there are the same number of molecules in 1g of methane and 2g of oxygen. This follows from the fact that the molecular mass of oxygen, 32, is twice that of methane, 16. Following this proportional relationship we can see that there will be the same number of molecules in 16g of methane and 32g of oxygen. In this case the number of grams of each substance has been chosen to be the same number as the molecular mass of the compound. The very large number of particles for which this is true is called **Avogadro's number**, after the man who first suggested how it could be estimated. The value of Avogadro's number is close to $6 \times 10^{23}$ (a six followed by twenty-three noughts).

It follows that $6 \times 10^{23}$ atoms of hydrogen will have a mass of 1g. As carbon has an atomic mass of 12, so $6 \times 10^{23}$ atoms of carbon will weigh 12g. That quantity of *any* compound which is the molecular mass in grams has a special name. It is called a *gram-molecule* or more often just a **mole**.

It is important that you appreciate that a *mole* of a chemical is a certain number (Avogadro's number) of molecules and hence, because molecules of different compounds have different masses, the *moles* of different compounds are also different masses. For instance, one mole of $CaCO_3$ has a mass of 100g, and one mole of $CaO$ has a mass of 56g.

To summarise, a balanced equation tells you first of all what are the smallest numbers of *molecules* of compounds which will react together. This is exactly the same as the number of *moles* of the compounds which react. Finally, now you can work out molecular masses (using Figure 3.7), you can work out how many *grams* of substances will react.

**Avogadro's number**

**mole**

*Worked Example*

What weight of quicklime can be slaked with a gallon (4.5 litres) of water?

The equation for slaking lime (mentioned earlier in section D1) is:

|  | $CaO$ | $+ H_2O$ | $\rightarrow Ca(OH)_2$ |
|---|---|---|---|
| in molecular masses: | 56 | $+ 18$ | $\rightarrow 74$ |
| in moles: | 1 mole | $+ 1$ mole | $\rightarrow 1$ mole |

Thus, if it can be determined how many moles of water are used, it will be known that the same number of moles of quicklime are slaked.

$$1 \text{ gallon of water} = 4.5 \text{ litres} = 4.5 \text{ kg} = 4500 \text{ g}$$

$$\text{As 1 mole of water is 18g, 4500g water is } \frac{4500}{18} = 250 \text{ moles}$$

From the chemical equation it can be seen that 250 moles of water will slake 250 moles of quicklime. 1 mole of quicklime is 56g, that is, its molecular mass in grams. Therefore the mass of lime which can be slaked is $250 \times 56\text{g} = 14{,}000\text{g}$ or 14 kilos.

### E3 Molar solutions

One circumstance in which you are quite likely to meet the idea of the mole is in expressing the strengths of solutions. If a litre of **molar solution** solution contains one mole of compound it is called a **molar solution**. A tenth molar solution consists of 0.1 moles in a litre of solution and would be written 0.1 M or M/10 to describe its strength. The molecular mass of sulphuric acid ($H_2SO_4$) is 98, as you can calculate. A solution of sulphuric acid at a strength of 98g per litre of *solution* would be a molar solution. Similarly, 9.8g of sulphuric acid added to water and made up to one litre would be an M/10 solution. The strength of a solution expressed in moles is called its **molarity** **molarity**.

You are probably used to referring to the strengths of solutions **concentration** (more properly called their **concentration**) in "weight per volume" terms, for example, 9.8 g/l. A fuller discussion of this and alternative terminologies is contained in Book II, but at this stage the advantages **molar concentration** of using the **molar concentration** description will be shown.

Consider the reaction of sulphuric acid and sodium hydroxide (an alkali) to form sodium sulphate and water.

$$H_2SO_4 + 2NaOH \rightarrow Na_2SO_4 + 2H_2O$$

You can see that 1 mole of the acid reacts with 2 moles of sodium hydroxide. When the reaction is complete, and there is no excess acid or alkali, the solution is called *neutral*. Given the *molar concentrations* of solutions of such compounds you can work out, for example, that a given volume of the acid at a given molar concentration will require exactly twice the volume of sodium hydroxide solution at the same molarity to produce a neutral solution. Or, again, equal volumes of solution will neutralise one another only if the sodium hydroxide is at *twice* the molarity of the acid. These are examples which further demonstrate that *a mole is a known number of molecules*. Neither example would be obvious in weight per volume terms: that 1 litre of 9.8g/l $H_2SO_4$ will neutralise 1 litre of 8.0g/l NaOH is not obvious, but that 1 litre of 0.1M (a tenth molar solution) sulphuric acid neutralises a litre of 0.2M solution follows from the chemical equation.

4

# Atomic structure and chemical bonding

# Atomic structure and chemical bonding

The idea that atoms are able to bond together to form molecules will be quite familiar to you by now. However, so far, nothing has been explained about *why* this should happen. By taking a closer look at the basic structure common to all atoms and then at their electrical properties it will become possible for you to see why atoms of one element behave in a different way to those of any other kind. This chapter will also explain the several different ways atoms can bond together, helping to reveal how this relates to a variety of physical and chemical properties displayed by the compounds and elements that you work with.

## A  The idea of valency

In the last chapter you learnt that the atomic mass of an element is one characteristic feature of its atoms. The structural formulae introduced in Chapter 3 revealed another characteristic; the number of links or bonds which one atom can make with others. The number of bonds that a single atom of an element can make is known as its **valency**. For many elements this is a constant number. The equation for the reaction which was used as an example earlier on

**valency**

$$CH_4 + 2O_2 \xrightarrow{\text{heat}} CO_2 + 2H_2O$$

the burning of methane gas, used four kinds of molecules with these structures:

**Figure 4.1**  *Structural formulae of molecules involved in the burning of natural gas.*

In these structures the number of dashes (which indicate bonds) emerging from each kind of atom is seen to be constant. Hydrogen is always joined to the next atom by one dash representing a single bond. Oxygen always makes two bonds and carbon always four. To indicate these characteristic numbers, the structures sometimes **double bond** show two bonds between one pair of atoms: a **double bond**.

You must remember, however, that the idea of constant valency is only a *model* and is not totally consistent (carbon monoxide is one example when it does not appear to work). However, for a wide range of compounds, especially organic ones, it is extremely useful. The following list provides the valency numbers for several elements commonly found in organic molecules.

**Valency**

| | H | F | Cl | Br |
|---|---|---|---|---|
| 1 | hydrogen | fluorine | chlorine | bromine |
| | O | S | | |
| 2 | oxygen | sulphur | | |
| | N | P | | |
| 3 | nitrogen | phosphorus | | |
| | C | | | |
| 4 | carbon | | | |

*Exercises*

1   Check the structural formulae of ethyl alcohol, dimethyl ether, ethylene oxide and acetaldehyde on page 47 in Chapter 3 to see that correct valencies have been used.

2   Draw structural formulae for the following molecules:

- **a**  $H_2$
- **b**  $N_2$
- **c**  $NH_3$  (ammonia)
- **d**  $CH_5N$  (methylamine)
- **e**  $C_2H_3Cl$  (vinyl chloride)
- **f**  The third isomer of $C_2H_4O$

Clearly these restrictions on how many bonds each kind of atom will make are the major influence in determining what proportions of different elements appear in any given compound. To understand the origin of the bonds and see why particular valency numbers occur for a given element, and to discover the limitations of this simple pattern-making exercise, more needs to be understood about what atoms themselves are made of.

# *B* The structure of atoms

## B1 The electrical connection

**static electricity**   You will, no doubt, be familiar with the effects of **static electricity** when polishing a glass case (or trying to wipe dust from a record). **forces of attraction**   As you polish, **forces of attraction** are built up between the case and the cloth, so that dust is often attracted to the surface you are trying to clean. Similarly, you may have noticed when undressing that some of your clothing (especially when made of synthetic fibres) sticks together, but may act as if repelled from another surface. These forces of attraction and repulsion are fundamental to the nature of electricity. The **electrostatic forces** produced by friction have been studied in great detail and it has been established that, as with magnetic forces, some of the forces attract and others repel. Objects are able to carry different amounts of electricity; the amount of electricity carried by a body is described as its **electric charge**. There are two kinds of electric charge. Objects with different (opposite) charges tend to attract one another, while those with like charges are repelled. It has also been observed that these forces of attraction and repulsion between electrified bodies rapidly decrease as the objects are moved further apart.

**electrostatic forces**

**electric charge**

Further research has established that atoms themselves are made up of electrified particles, some carrying charge of one kind and some of the other. These two types of electricity are denoted by the terms **positive ( + )** and **negative ( − )**. When electrification through friction takes place, a few of these minute particles become transferred from one atom to another, so that the normal even mixture of the positive and negative particles amongst atoms is distorted. A dominance of one or other type is created, causing an overall positive or negative charge to occur on the rubbed surface.

**positive ( + ),
negative ( − )**

## B2 The composition of atoms

There are two kinds of **charged particles** in atoms:

**charged particles**

*Protons*    which carry a positive electric charge and have almost the same mass as a hydrogen atom

*Electrons*    which carry an electric charge of exactly the same "strength" as that on the protons but negative in kind. They are very much lighter, only 1/2000th the mass of a hydrogen atom.

Atoms also contain a third type of particle:

*Neutrons*    so called because they are electrically neutral (carrying no charge). They have about the same mass as protons (they are very slightly heavier).

In the past the structure of atoms has been compared to the solar system of the sun and planets. At the centre of an atom is a **nucleus** which contains only the heavy particles (protons and neutrons). Just as the sun contains almost all the mass in the solar system, so the nucleus of an atom contains almost all the mass of the atom.

**nucleus**

Individual atoms (helium, oxygen, neon, etc.) are electrically neutral and so for every proton in the nucleus there must be a balancing negative electric charge. This is provided by the electrons which envelop the nucleus. There is the same number of electrons as there are protons. The electrons are in constant motion around the nucleus, which can be paralleled by the motion of planets around the sun. The sun attracts the planets orbiting it by gravitational force and, in a comparable way, the nucleus holds on to its electrons by an *electrostatic* force. This force is attractive because electrons and protons have opposite charges.

The analogy with the solar system cannot be taken very far. In an atom, the electrons are moving very fast and the whole system is extremely small. It is not possible to say precisely where each electron is at any one time. It is much more realistic, therefore, to think of a fuzzy, roughly spherical volume of space surrounding the nucleus in which all the electrons can be found but not precisely **electron cloud** located. This is often described as the **electron cloud**.

This model of an atom can help you to understand much more about the behaviour of atoms. It suggests, for example, that the chemistry of an atom is connected more with the electron cloud than the nucleus. It is the electron clouds which form the outer parts of atoms and, consequently, come into contact with one another when atoms collide. It is also in accord with the visual model of a molecule given at the beginning of Chapter 3 where it was suggested that atoms, joined together to form a molecule, merge into each other. This is, of course, easy to imagine if the outer parts of the atom are cloud-like rather than rigid. However, this visualisation of the atom will have to be developed further still to explain why colliding atoms sometimes bond together to make molecules, and at others bounce apart.

Although there are about a hundred distinct types of atoms, they are all composed of these three fundamental particles. The difference between atoms is in the number of particles present within them.

## B3 The atomic nucleus, mass numbers and isotopes

It has been emphasised just how invisibly small whole atoms are, but the nucleus of an atom is small even in comparison with an atom — less than one thousandth of the atomic diameter. Into this tiny **protons** volume are packed **protons** (particles with positive electric charges). The forces of repulsion between them are very great and so there has to be some other force holding them together. This is a role of the **neutrons** **neutrons** and (except for hydrogen which has a nucleus with only one proton) all atomic nuclei contain neutrons.

All elements are chemically different from each other and it has gradually emerged that the chemical behaviour of an element is governed by the number of electrons that surround the nucleus. For the electric charges within an atom to balance there must be the same number of electrons outside as there are protons inside the nucleus. Consequently, a feature which distinguishes atoms of one element from another is the *number of protons* in the nucleus. Each different element has a specific number of protons. Hydrogen, the lightest atom has only one; helium, the next in weight, has two; lithium has three and so on, up to the heaviest naturally occurring element, uranium, which has 92. The number of protons in an atom's nucleus **atomic number** is called its **atomic number** and is a specific and systematic way of identifying an element.

The number of neutrons in the nucleus is about the same as the number of protons, although the proportion of neutrons increases in the heavier elements. In hydrogen there are *no* neutrons; in helium there are two protons and two neutrons; in aluminium there are 13 protons and 14 neutrons; in the heavy element, gold, there are 79 protons and 118 neutrons.

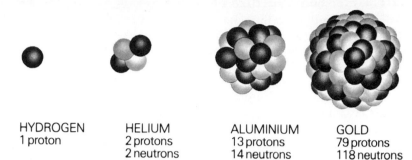

| HYDROGEN | HELIUM | ALUMINIUM | GOLD |
|---|---|---|---|
| 1 proton | 2 protons | 13 protons | 79 protons |
| | 2 neutrons | 14 neutrons | 118 neutrons |

**Figure 4.2** *Pictorial representation of the nuclei of various atoms.*

The number of protons is constant and specific for any element. However, for many elements, the nuclei of atoms of that particular element do not always have the same number of neutrons. For example, the nuclei of atoms of copper which all contain 29 protons, can have either 34 or 36 neutrons in them. Since the electrons in an atom are so very small and light compared with the nucleus, and since protons and neutrons have masses very close to one "hydrogen atom unit", (Chapter 3, section E) the total mass of the atom can be fairly accurately calculated by adding the number of protons to the number of neutrons. This gives a whole number called the **mass number**. The two forms of copper atom have mass numbers of 63 and 65 (29 + 34 and 29 + 36). These different forms of the same element are called **isotopes**. In nature, copper occurs as a mixture of its two isotopes; the lighter isotope is more than twice as common as the heavier. In a sample of copper metal or in a copper corrosion product, the two kinds of atom will be completely mixed and there is no way of separating them chemically. If calculations related to chemical reactions are used to determine the atomic mass of copper, the answer will come out as an average between the two. In tables of accurate atomic mass that of copper is listed as 63.54 whereas any individual atom will have an atomic mass which is very nearly a whole number.

**mass number**

**isotopes**

In writing, isotopes are distinguished by adding a **superscript** to the symbol for that element. The isotope of carbon with six protons and six neutrons is called $^{12}C$. (This is the standard by which, in accurate work, all other atomic masses are judged nowadays.) The isotope of carbon with six protons and eight neutrons is called $^{14}C$. The nuclei in $^{14}C$ are unstable and liable to disintegrate. So the proportions of stable $^{12}C$ and unstable $^{14}C$ change with time. This is the basis of $^{14}C$ dating. If during conservation treatment a carbon-containing material is introduced into an object, for example as a

**superscript**

consolidant in rotten wood, the ratio of the $^{14}C$ and $^{12}C$ isotopes which is characteristic of the age of the original organic material will be distorted, because the new material will have a different age and so a different **isotope ratio**. As a conservator, you should be aware that archaeometric evidence will thus be destroyed.

**isotope ratio**

### B4 The electron structure of atoms

Early attempts to describe what goes on within the electron cloud visualised electrons as circling the nucleus in predictable orbits just as planets progress around the sun. It is now known that it is impossible to be so sure what the position, speed and direction of travel of an electron is at any particular moment. All one can hope to do is to specify a volume of space around the nucleus and say that there is a high chance of finding the electron in that space. These volumes of space are called **orbitals**. There are orbitals around the nucleus of every atom. Some orbitals have electrons in them and some may be empty. Each orbital can contain two electrons; so carbon which has six electrons has three filled orbitals, and gold with 79 electrons has 39 filled orbitals and one that is half filled.

**orbitals**

In the light elements the filled orbitals are small but in the heavier elements much larger orbitals are full. This means that there is a greater probability of finding electrons further away from the nucleus. Put simply, this means that the atoms of heavy elements are larger than those of light ones; an atom of gold has a diameter about twice that of a carbon atom.

Orbitals have many different shapes; those of the heavier elements are quite complicated. These complex shapes penetrate into one another. Despite this complexity, the overall effect is that the greatest density of electrons is found in concentric spherical *shells* surrounding the nucleus. This **shell structure** is shown in Figure 4.3 in two different forms.

**shell structure**

**Figure 4.3a**  *Cross-section of the electron cloud, in two dimensions, showing the three "shells" of greatest electron density.*

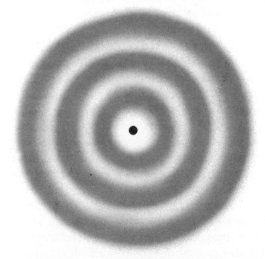

**Figure 4.3b**   *Three-dimensional representation of 4.3a, showing the shells inside each other.*

The innermost shells will nearly always be completely filled. The outermost shell may be full, nearly full, half empty or almost empty. It is these four rough categories which determine the chemical character of an element.

Atoms in which the outermost shell of orbitals is completely full are very stable. Of particular significance in determining chemical behaviour is a **filled outer shell** containing eight electrons – a condition which many atoms will try to achieve through chemical reaction. There are five elements whose atoms do not enter into any chemical reactions. These atoms have totally filled outer-most shells and can collide with other atoms and molecules without reacting with them. These elements are neon, argon, krypton, xenon and radon, which are gases found in the atmosphere in small amounts and are known as the *rare* or **inert gases**.

The principle of **bonding** is that atoms can share or swap electrons between outer shells to achieve the stable condition of eight electrons in their outermost shells. Atoms involved in these exchanges then stay close together forming molecules. (Hydrogen and helium atoms, however, do not fit this pattern of eight, as the first orbital shell – the shell which is closest to the nucleus – is filled by only two electrons.)

To understand chemistry you have to look further at the way in which atoms acquire stability. They do this through "giving", "taking" or "sharing" the electrons occupying their outermost shells with other atoms to achieve a full complement of eight electrons in their outer shells. Which of these methods is used depends on how many electrons the atom has in its outermost shell to begin with. Atoms which have a nearly empty shell of electrons will readily give electrons away leaving the underlying full shell. Atoms with a nearly full shell will readily accept electrons to make up the full number. In between, the atoms with half-filled outer shells will tend to share electrons.

**filled outer shell**

**inert gases**

**bonding**

These properties can be illustrated most clearly by considering the twenty lightest elements. Figure 4.4 shows their names, symbols, and the number of electrons they contain.

| Number of electrons in atom | Name of element | Symbol | Notes |
|:---:|:---|:---:|:---|
| 1 | hydrogen | H | 1st shell incomplete |
| 2 | helium | He | 1st shell full |
| 3 | lithium | Li | 2nd shell incomplete |
| 4 | beryllium | Be | |
| 5 | boron | B | |
| 6 | carbon | C | |
| 7 | nitrogen | N | |
| 8 | oxygen | O | |
| 9 | fluorine | F | |
| 10 | neon | Ne | 1st and 2nd shells full |
| 11 | sodium | Na | 3rd shell incomplete |
| 12 | magnesium | Mg | |
| 13 | aluminium | Al | |
| 14 | silicon | Si | |
| 15 | phosphorus | P | |
| 16 | sulphur | S | |
| 17 | chlorine | Cl | |
| 18 | argon | A | 1st, 2nd and 3rd shells full |
| 19 | potassium | K | 4th shell incomplete |
| 20 | calcium | Ca | |

**Figure 4.4** *Table demonstrating the degree to which the electron shells are filled for the highest elements.*

If these elements are grouped according to how many electrons they have in their outermost shells (and hydrogen is omitted because of its exceptional structure), one starts to make a **periodic table** (Figure 4.5). The elements in each column not only have the same number of electrons in the outer shell but also show similar chemical properties. The pattern within the periodic table was recognised long before anyone could explain it in terms of the electron structure of atoms. You will become aware of some of the similarities amongst elements and their compounds which the table shows.

**periodic table**

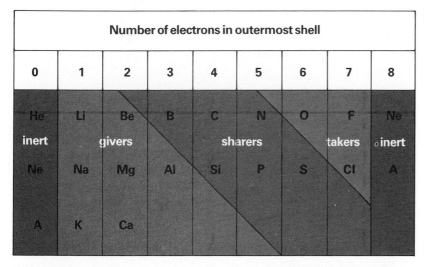

| Number of electrons in outermost shell | | | | | | | | |
|---|---|---|---|---|---|---|---|---|
| 0 | 1 | 2 | 3 | 4 | 5 | 6 | 7 | 8 |
| He | Li | Be | B | C | N | O | F | Ne |
| inert | givers | | | sharers | | | takers | inert |
| Ne | Na | Mg | Al | Si | P | S | Cl | A |
| A | K | Ca | | | | | | |

**Figure 4.5** *Partial periodic table. Ne and A (inert gases) can be seen as having eight electrons in one shell or none in the next, and appear twice.*

For elements heavier than calcium the regularity of the periodic pattern is distorted. Look at the full periodic table at the back of this book. Although it is not regular, the full periodic table can still be explained systematically in terms of the numbers of electrons in different types of orbital. To explain the mechanisms of valency, without too much complication, only the first two rows of the table will be used here.

Looking again at Figure 4.5, you will see that shading has been used to show which elements are electron givers, sharers or takers. The ways in which bonds are formed vary according to which of these classes of atoms are brought together. Several types of combination will be looked at in turn.

# C Bonding mechanisms

## C1 Covalency: bonding by sharing

Methane is a molecule containing two elements each with atoms possessing half-full outermost electron shells. It is an example of a molecule made by atoms sharing electrons. Bonds formed by this mechanism are called **covalent bonds**.

**covalent bonds**

Figure 4.6 represents the atoms of hydrogen and carbon diagramatically, showing the electron shells and the electrons.

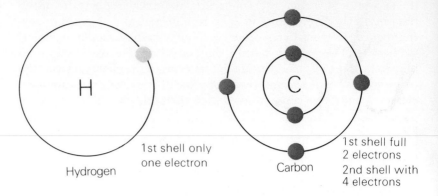

**Figure 4.6**

You will notice that the electrons in the two atoms have been represented by two different symbols. This has been done purely to illustrate the origin of the electrons when full shells have been formed by sharing. It is important to remember, however, that they are in reality identical. Figure 4.7 shows a model of the methane molecule, demonstrating the origin of the electrons forming the bonds between the atoms. The first shell of each hydrogen atom is made complete by sharing one electron from the carbon. The first shell of the carbon atom is already full. The second shell of carbon is made up to its full complement of eight electrons by sharing one electron from each hydrogen atom.

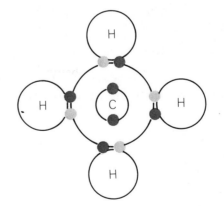

**Figure 4.7**

These models are not drawn in exactly the same way in every book you read but you will always be able to see shared electrons. A common form for diagrams such as these suppresses the superfluous information about the inner full shells and presents methane as shown in Figure 4.8 (a).

Here the rings are used merely to enclose electrons shared by each atom. Once the molecule is formed, the origin of any individual

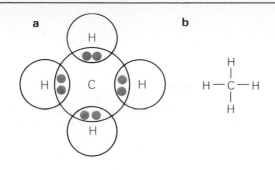

**Figure 4.8**

electron is unimportant and cannot be determined, so distinct symbols are quite meaningless. The shared electrons are therefore all shown by the same symbol, dots, in Figure 4.8 (a). It is now obvious why the valency of carbon is always four and the valency of hydrogen is always one.

You can see that all five atoms have achieved full outer shells, and consequently there is no tendency for any more electron swapping or sharing to occur. The whole group "looks" like an inert gas atom with a stable electron arrangement of full shells.

As a result, these molecules can endure rapid movement and collisions without undergoing chemical change. Only a collision which is violent enough to break the sharing bonds will provoke a chemical reaction.

If you compare the new picture of methane, Figure 4.8 (a), with the structural formula, Figure 4.8 (b), you can see that the bond shown by one dash means the sharing of a pair of electrons between the atoms. The covalent bond is called an **electron-pair bond**.

**electron-pair bond**

Electron models corresponding to other structural formulae can be drawn. Two are shown in Figure 4.9. In Figure 4.9 (b) you should pay attention to the "double" bond between the carbon atoms which represents *two* pairs of electrons being shared by two atoms.

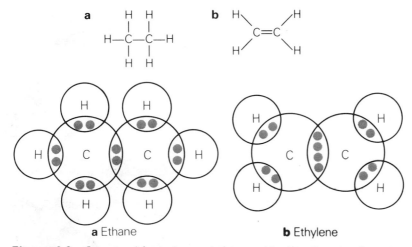

**a** Ethane          **b** Ethylene

**Figure 4.9**  *Structural formulae and electron-sharing diagrams for two more compounds of carbon and hydrogen.*

*Exercises*

3 Construct electron-sharing pictures for (a) ammonia, $NH_3$;
(b) nitrogen, $N_2$; and (c) methylamine, $CH_3NH_2$.

To do this you will first have to construct an electron model for
a nitrogen atom. Consult the periodic table (figure 4.5) to remind
yourself how many electrons a nitrogen atom has. Check that in your
complete molecules each H atom has a share of two electrons and
other types of atoms have shares of eight electrons.

---

Another value of these models is that they show that each atom
in a molecule is "satisfied" with its complement of electrons without
any atom receiving or losing any electrical charge. This fact means
that the molecules have little tendency to stick together having
become almost like the atoms of the inert gases. The consequence is
that covalently bonded molecular compounds, unless of high
molecular weight, *tend* to have low melting points, and to form
mobile liquids and weak, easily distorted solids (eg plastics). You
must note, however, that the word "tend" denotes a range of
behaviour that is very, very wide.

### Electron takers in covalent bonds

When you studied the reaction of methane with oxygen you noted
that oxygen occurs in O molecules. However, oxygen would rather
take electrons than share them. If there are no other atoms nearby
which will *give* electrons, one oxygen atom will share electrons with
another forming an oxygen molecule. Covalent sharing is the mutually satisfying answer and oxygen molecules form as in Figure 4.10
where the electrons of the two atoms are distinguished to show what
is going on. You can see that according to the pattern of bonding so
far developed, this must be a double bond as in Figure 4.1.

**Figure 4.10**

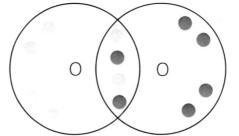

**Figure 4.11**

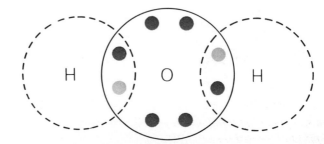

Opposite is a representation of the arrangement of electrons in a water molecule (Figure 4.11). This appears as straightforward covalency but the oxygen atom is so demanding of electrons that the molecule is most stable when the oxygen atom attracts the hydrogen atoms' electrons towards itself. The positive hydrogen nuclei (protons) are therefore exposed and the oxygen atom has a slight negative charge because of the extra share of negative electrons. An added important factor is that the directions of the bonds the oxygen atom will make are not diametrically opposite as drawn but are at slightly more than a right angle (108°) to each other. This is because, as with the methane molecule, the hydrogen atoms and the non-bonding electrons (the four outer shell electrons not involved in the electron pair bonds) achieve an arrangement where they are as far apart as possible. A truer representation of the water molecule is therefore like that shown in Figure 4.12.

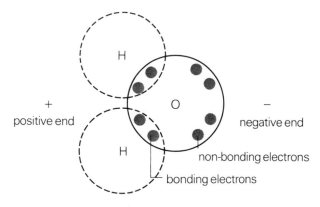

**Figure 4.12**

The similarity to the tetrahedral structure of methane is better shown in another representation (Figure 4.13) where the non-bonding electron pairs are shown in directional orbital lobes.

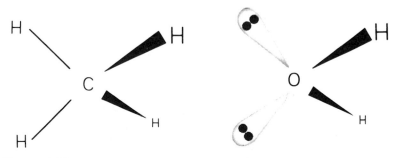

**Figure 4.13**

A molecule which has two separate but opposite particle charges on it is called *polar*. The **polarity** of water has a profound effect upon its properties, making it a useful solvent. (See Book II.)

**polarity**

**dative bond**

### Covalent bonds which are "dative"

It is also possible for atoms to make sharing bonds in which both the electrons involved in a bond originate from only one of the atoms. Such a bond used to be known as a **dative**, meaning "giving".

Sulphur dioxide is a pollutant of the air which causes acid attack on masonry. Its molecular formula is $SO_2$. Both kinds of atoms in the molecule have outer shells containing six electrons. The sulphur atom is known to lie between the oxygen atoms. Figure 4.14 is a possible electron structure which obeys the "rule of eight" (having an outer "complete" shell of eight electrons).

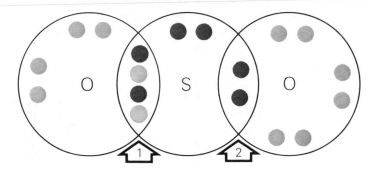

**Figure 4.14**   *An attempt to make the "rule of eight" work for $SO_2$.*

The bond labelled 1 is an ordinary double covalent bond exactly paralleling the central bond in ethylene (Figure 4.9 (b)), but the bond marked 2 is different. To make the model of the rule of eight work, both the electrons in this bond have to be described as coming from the sulphur atom, which is why it is called a "dative" bond.

### Molecular orbitals

However, experiment has shown that the bonds between oxygen and sulphur in sulphur dioxide are identical, and not one single and one double as the model suggests. Thus, in more modern theories, the bonding of molecules such as $SO_2$ is explained more accurately by considering an electron cloud for the whole molecule. Just as there are *atomic orbitals* which are stable zones for electrons surrounding the one nucleus of a single atom, so there are **molecular orbitals** which are stable electron arrangements surrounding the several nuclei of a molecule. Thus, a new diagram for $SO_2$ could be visualised as Figure 4.15.

**molecular orbitals**

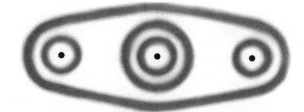

**Figure 4.15** *Molecular orbitals of a three-atom molecule in cross-section showing a cloud of outer electrons under the influence of all three nuclei, and the inner electron clouds under the influence of a single nucleus.*

Similar molecular orbital diagrams could be drawn for all the small molecules that we have considered such as oxygen and methane. Molecular orbitals can be thought of as being formed by the overlapping of the atomic orbitals; the merging of the electron clouds.

The eight-electron rule does not accurately predict all the properties of simple molecules. However, the mathematics involved in the more complete molecular orbital theory is very complicated and it cannot provide so simple and useful a guide to molecular structure as the rule of eight.

## C2 Ions: bonding by electron transfer

Metals form compounds with other elements by a mechanism which, although it can be viewed as a logical extension of covalency, is really quite different. Such compounds are relevant to conservation in many ways. Many artefacts are made of compounds of metals; for instance ceramics, glass, and stone contain combined metals. The corrosion of metals is caused by the formation of similar compounds. The effectiveness of various electrolytic methods of stabilising corrosion entirely depends on the nature of this bonding mechanism.

The periodic table (Figure 4.5) shows that the atoms of metals (eg Li, Na, K) have only a few electrons in excess of a stable inert gas structure. The basis of the **ionic bonding** system is that metal atoms acquire the stable outer shell of eight electrons by completely shedding those few extra electrons. There must be somewhere for the electrons to go. You may well have deduced that the lost electrons go to the outer orbitals of atoms which need to *accept* a few electrons in order to reach the stable eight-electron configuration. Oxygen and chlorine are two common elements found in this role and the compounds which are formed when such an exchange of electrons has occurred are known respectively as **oxides** and **chlorides**.

The atoms involved in these exchanges become electrically charged because an imbalance in the numbers of electrons and protons is created through loss or gain of electrons. The charged atoms are known as **ions**. The elements which readily lose electrons (metals) are called **electropositive** because the ions they form have a positive charge – the result of shedding negative electrons. The loss of electrons can be written as a chemical equation in the following way:

| Cu | – | $e^-$ | → | $Cu^+$ |
|----|---|-------|---|--------|
| copper atom | take away | a negatively charged electron | becomes | a positively charged copper ion |

**ionic bonding**

**oxides and chlorides**

**ions**
**electropositive**

Positive ions are also known as **cations** (*cat*–ions) because in electrolysis they migrate to the *cathode* (the end connected to the negative pole of the battery which, of course, attracts positive particles). (See Book II.)

**cations**

Negative ions, **anions** (*an*–ions) (which are attracted to the positive *anode* during electrolysis) are formed from **electronegative atoms** which collect the electrons lost by metal atoms. In an equation the change can be written as a reaction between an atom and one or more electrons:

**anions**
**electronegative atoms**

$$Cl \quad + \quad e^- \quad \rightarrow \quad Cl^-$$

chlorine     negatively charged     negatively charged
atom     electron     chloride ion

$$O \quad + \quad 2e^- \quad \rightarrow \quad O^{2-}$$

oxygen atom     *two* negative     oxide ion carrying *two*
electrons     electrons' worth of charge

In these equations you will have noticed ions written as the atomic symbols carrying + and − signs. The convention is that the number of electrons lost or gained by an atom in becoming an ion is shown as a superscript to the element symbol with a plus or minus next to it to show the residual charge. Thus a chloride ion, $Cl^-$, is a chlorine atom which has accepted one electron, the oxide ion $O^{2-}$ carries two extra electrons. Similarly, the copper ion $Cu^+$ is a copper atom which has lost one electron (known as a cupr*ous* ion), while another condition of ionised copper, $Cu^{2+}$, is *two* electrons short of being a complete atom. This state is known as the cupr*ic* ion. By analogy with the number of bonds an atom forms in a covalent compound, **ionic valency** the number of charges on an atom is called its **valency**. So $Cu^{2+}$ is called two-valent. These names are further explained in the next chapter.

Ions need not only be single atoms with an excess or deficit of charge. Anions in particular occur as clusters of atoms which are as stable as molecules but are charged. You will meet many examples in the following chapter but among compounds already mentioned white lead pigment contains $OH^-$ ions (hydroxide) and $CO_3^{2-}$ ions (carbonate). Gesso, calcium sulphate, contains $SO_4^{2-}$ ions.

Once ions of opposite charge are formed by the transfer of electrons from one atom to another there will be an electrostatic force of attraction between them. It is this force which constitutes the **ionic bond**. Moreover, because of the non-directional nature of electrostatic forces it becomes meaningless to talk of a "molecule" of an ionic compound. In the first section of this chapter the number of bonds one atom could make to others (valency) was mentioned and it was seen in discussing the mechanism of covalency how that number was limited. Charged ions of one sign, in contrast, will attract *any* ions of opposite sign and from any direction causing every ion to be surrounded by oppositely charged ions. Equally, ions of the same sign repel one another and so structures develop where these attractive and repulsive forces are so organised that **crystals** there is a net attractive force. The result is the **crystals** of metal compounds whose regular shapes reflect an orderly arrangement of positive and negative ions each surrounded by neighbours of opposite sign. More will be said about crystals in Section D of this chapter but meanwhile let us look at what has happened to the idea of molecules in such a compound.

If you make some quicklime (CaO) by roasting limestone you will end up with a white powder. Each particle of the powder must contain billions of ions of two kinds, $Ca^{2+}$ and $O^{2-}$, in equal numbers. Each calcium atom has two electrons to give and each oxygen atom will accept two. In three dimensions the assembly is a crystal; the diagram (Figure 4.16) shows a two-dimensional representation of the alternation of positive and negative ions:

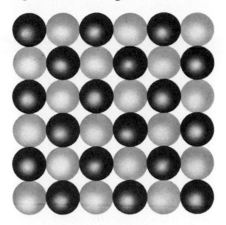

**Figure 4.16**

What can the idea of a molecule mean in such a continuous structure? Take one of the calcium ions near the middle of the picture. Is the "molecule" CaO:

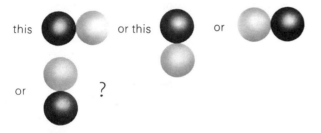

Each ion is surrounded by a number of oppositely charged ions and is not associated with any one in particular. Each little crystal has grown from an embryo of just a few ions but it is most unlikely that every crystal will be the same size. The formula of an ionic compound such as CaO means something different from the formula for a covalent one. With a covalent compound the formula shows the particular grouping of atoms which stick together as a molecule but for an ionic compound it merely tells the relative proportions of elements which exist in the substance. For this reason it is more correct to speak of **formula mass** than *molecular mass*, though this is a little pedantic and certainly you will find the term *molecular mass* (or of course *molecular weight*) used for ionic materials.

**formula mass**

## C3 Bonding in metals

Most metals, as you know, are strong solid materials at ordinary temperatures. We have to find an explanation for the fact that these atoms, all of one kind, which all want to lose electrons to establish an inert structure, are found bonded together. The mechanism is similar to the molecular orbital idea which was used to explain sulphur dioxide.

**metallic bond**

If electrons can be distributed over more than two atoms to form a bond then it is not too difficult to suppose that electrons can mutually belong to thousands of atoms. Metal atoms carry just a few electrons in their outermost orbitals. As the atoms are packed together into a solid, these sparsely populated outer orbitals readily overlap and the electrons which they contain cease to ''belong'' to any particular atom.

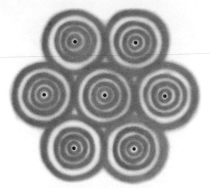

**Figure 4.17**  *Electron sharing among several metal atoms.*

The electrons can thus move freely from one atom to another because none of the overlapping outer orbitals is full. In other words, the outer electrons belong to all the atoms. The mobile electrons act as a cohesive force preventing the positive metal ions from pushing each other apart. Just as with the ionic bond there is no distinct group of atoms which can be identified as a molecule. This type of structure can extend indefinitely in any direction. Often the most stable structure (and hence the most likely one) will be that in which there is the greatest overlap of the orbitals of one atom with those of its neighbours. This is achieved in many metals (such as copper, silver, and gold) by a regular pattern called close-packing. The regular array of repeating units in three dimensions suggests that metals are crystalline. It is unusual to see individual metal crystals in isolation, but solid metal objects are made up of large numbers of small crystals joined together. The boundaries between these crystals can be seen under a microscope.

**Figure 4.18**  *Photomicrograph, showing the individual crystals in a sample of brass – 60% copper, 40% zinc.*

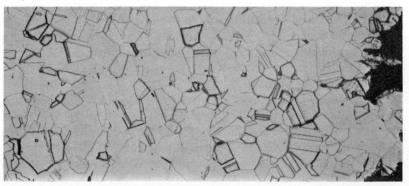

*Three types of bond?*

Covalent, ionic and metallic bonds have been described as if they formed three distinct categories. We have seen that really these three are just definable points in a wide range of bonding behaviour.

Covalent bonding describes not only the equal sharing of an electron pair between two atoms but may involve electron sharing over larger numbers of atoms (as in $SO_2$). The extreme form of this is the completely delocalised electron structure of metals.

In a covalent bond the electrons may not be shared equally between the atoms if one is more electronegative than another (oxygen in $H_2O$). The extreme form of unequal sharing is when there is complete electron transfer from one atom to another, as is found in the ionic bond.

# D Physical properties related to bonding

The materials of which objects are made have different physical characteristics which distinguish them from each other. Materials are often chosen for a particular job because of these distinguishing features. Copper, which conducts electricity well, is used in wires to carry current, while plastics such as polyvinyl chloride, which do not conduct electricity, are used as insulation for the copper wire. Solvents with low boiling points are used for dry-cleaning because they will evaporate rapidly from the textile, once the cleaning has been finished.

The range of possible properties is very great. Materials may be heavy, light, opaque, transparent, volatile, involatile, rigid, fluid, electrically conductive, non-conductive. Many of these properties can be directly related to the kind of bonding within the material. If you ask four questions about the physical properties of a particular material, you will find that it can be placed in one of four classes, which, broadly speaking, indicate four different types of bonding and structure.

The questions are:
1 Are the temperatures at which the material melts and boils low or high? (A convenient dividing line is 200°C for the boiling point. Many substances will decompose above this temperature rather than melt or boil, but even so they still belong in the high temperature class since they do not change state at a temperature below 200°C.)
2 Can the material be made to conduct electricity freely?
3 Does the material conduct electricity in both the solid and the liquid states?
4 Does it only conduct electricity in the liquid state, that is when molten, or when dissolved in a liquid?

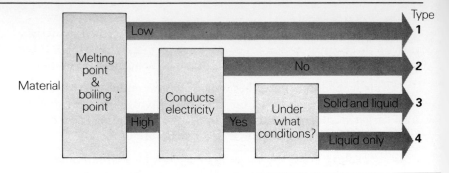

**Figure 4.19**  *Flowchart to separate materials into the four types.*

The first two groups in the diagram are covalently bonded materials while three and four are metallic and ionic ones.

## Type 1: Materials with low boiling points

In a gas or vapour the particles are in rapid and random motion – there cannot be any very strong links or attractive forces between them or they would stay close together. If a liquid readily becomes a vapour without one having to do a lot of work on it, then the links between the particles cannot be very strong in the liquid state either. If you have to heat a liquid strongly before it will become a vapour then the particles must be held together fairly strongly.

**volatile compounds**  **Volatile compounds** such as acetone or alcohol can be distilled. They evaporate and condense but still remain the same compounds. This means that although the links between the molecules are very weak, the links between the atoms within the molecules must be strong and not easily broken.

This condition is just what you would expect of the molecules of covalently bonded substances. Electronically, all the molecules are well satisfied, as the mechanism which holds the atoms together has left no tendency for further joining. The molecules are electronically neutral since they are composed of neutral atoms; the total number of electrons balances the total number of protons in any one particle. For a material to conduct electricity there must be movement of electrically charged particles, eg ions or electrons. As these covalent molecules are neutral, moving them about does not cause any movement of electric charge and so these substances are not conductors of electricity.

Light molecules move more easily than heavier ones. We would expect materials with low molecular mass to have lower boiling points than those with high molecular mass, as the heavy molecules will need more heat to get them moving fast enough to become a gas. This trend is shown in the following table.

| Substance | Molecular Mass | Boiling Point °C |
|---|---|---|
| hydrogen | 2 | −253 |
| nitrogen | 28 | −196 |
| carbon dioxide | 44 | − 78 |
| diethyl ether | 74 | + 35 |
| toluene | 92 | +111 |

The fact that covalent substances can exist as liquids and solids as well as gases must mean that there are *some* forces of attraction between molecules. These are weak compared to the bonds between atoms in molecules and so are called **secondary bonds**. These forces often cause dirt to stick to objects (see Book II) and they account for the adhesion of glues (see Book III). For now, it is enough to be aware that forces weaker than the **primary bonds** (forces of attraction *within* molecules) do exist and that they, too, cover a range of strengths. These forces hold polar molecules together. This is why substances with polar molecules such as water and ethyl alcohol, which are liquid at room temperature, need more heat put into them to make them boil than do substances of similar or greater molecular mass which have non-polar molecules (eg nitrogen, oxygen and carbon dioxide).

**secondary bonds**

**primary bonds**

*Type 2: Non-volatile materials which do not conduct electricity*
It is unusual for a compound with molecules containing more than 40 atoms, or which has a molecular mass greater than 350, to be volatile. There is, however, no restriction on the size of covalent molecules and natural and synthetic polymers such as protein and polythene may have molecular masses of many hundreds of thousands. Often such **large molecules** are made up by repeating relatively simple units in the form of a chain (eg polyvinyl acetate). There is then a range of possible molecular masses because the number of repeat units can vary from molecule to molecule. Molecular formulae such as $(CH_3COOCHCH_2)_n$ can be used to show that a large but uncertain number of units is repeated. A great many materials used in conservation are composed of giant covalent molecules; wool, silk, cotton, polyester thread, wood, leather, PVA, nylon, Perspex (Plexiglass), etc. The molecules of cellulose in cotton are composed of about 3000 repeated units each containing 21 atoms. Here is part of its structure:

**chain molecules**

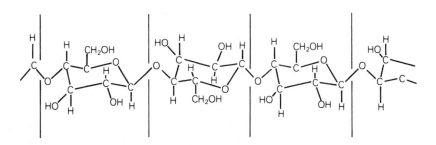

**Figure 4.20** *Part of the structural formula for cellulose $(C_6H_{10}O_5)_n$, showing how the units repeat.*

Materials with such big molecules cannot evaporate easily. The long chains may actually become physically tangled. When the material is heated the primary bonds are eventually broken and chemical changes such as charring are frequently observed.

The properties of a substance composed of large covalent molecules will depend very much on their size and shape. If the molecules are relatively compact, they will stack together neatly and regularly in the solid and will form hard crystals (like sugar). If they are long twisting string-like molecules, they will tend to lie lengthways alongside one another but not necessarily in any orderly fashion. In this case, the solid may be very flexible and have strong directional properties. Examples are the fibres of wood and silk.

Diamond is a poor conductor of electricity and is not at all volatile. It can be burned at extremely high temperatures in oxygen to form carbon dioxide and nothing else. This expensive experiment shows that diamond is composed of nothing but carbon atoms and is chemically identical to the black carbon we are familiar with in charcoal and carbon inks. If the carbon atoms were not joined to one another in any way, we would expect it (with molecular mass as low as 12) to be very volatile, even gaseous, at room temperature (compare nitrogen which has a molecular mass of 28); but diamond is hard and crystalline with a melting point in excess of 3500°C. The molecule of diamond must be very big; what is its structure? If it contains covalent bonds the diamond molecule will contain carbon atoms with a valency of 4. There are several ways that large numbers of carbon atoms could be joined together so that each has four bonds attached to it. (Try to see how many you can find.) The rigidity and symmetry of diamond suggests that there are not long flexible strings of carbon atoms or large flat sheet-like molecules that could slide over one another. The actual structure in some ways resembles that of methane, where the C—H bonds point to the corners of an imaginary tetrahedron. The diamond "molecule" is an infinite three-dimensional **lattice** of carbon atoms each joined by four tetrahedrally arranged bonds to four other carbon atoms.

**lattice**

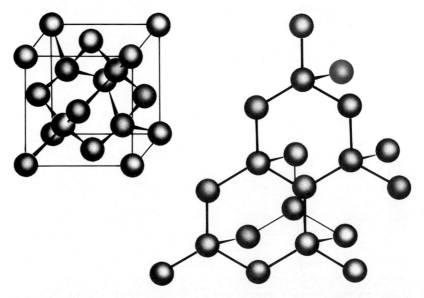

**Figure 4.21**  *Two representations of the structure of diamond.*

This structure exists throughout a single piece of the solid and so it does not form a molecule in the sense discussed so far. For this reason, the word *molecule* is seldom used for such giant three-dimensional arrays. (Graphite, another form of carbon which is soft and readily conducts electricity, has a very different structure from diamond and will be dealt with under Type 3.) Thermosetting polymers like the casting resins or Bakelite form similar continuous three-dimensional covalently bonded structures.

Silica is another of these infinite covalent lattices. It is composed of silicon atoms combined with twice the number of oxygen atoms. Since the elements are in the ratio 1:2 it is given the formula $SiO_2$, but this does not imply that there are individual $SiO_2$ molecules. Silica can have several structures, quartz being one of them. In all the structures the silicon-oxygen bonds are tetrahedrally arranged and there is an oxygen atom between any two silicon atoms. (Silicon has a valency of four and oxygen a valency of two.) These materials are non-conductors of electricity, that is, insulators. This is because the particles are not free to move in the rigid bonding framework. The electrons are all involved in bonding and the atoms are neutral.

### Type 3: Materials with high melting points which conduct electricity in the solid state

Materials with high melting temperatures which conduct electricity in the solid state must have strong bonds holding the atoms together, but there must also be some freely mobile electrically charged particles. Most such materials are metals: the previous description of the metallic bond (see page 79) fulfils these requirements. The atoms are held tightly together by the overlap of their orbitals. Those electrons which become the common property of all the atoms can readily move within the metal under the action of any electric driving force (ie a voltage). Other properties of metals, such as their lustre and good conductivity of heat, can also be explained in terms of this bonding structure. The ductility and malleability of metals like copper, silver and gold are related to the way the atoms are stacked

**Figure 4.22** *Photomicrograph of cold-worked brass. Compare the deformed crystal structure here with Figure 4.18.*

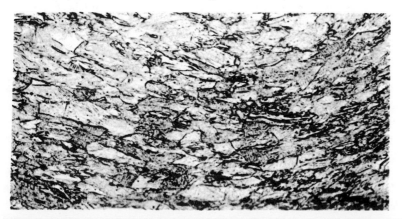

together in the crystals. Even simple spherical atoms can be arranged regularly in three dimensions in several different ways. The atoms in ductile metals are aligned in planes. There is no strong bonding directly between any two atoms so large groups of atoms can move relative to one another along these planes without breaking any specific bonds. When this happens the crystals become deformed as in Figure 4.22.

**graphite**    **Graphite**, one of the forms in which carbon is found, has a structure which has some similarity to that of the metals. The carbon atoms are joined by covalent bonds into planar networks of hexagonal rings (Figure 4.23).

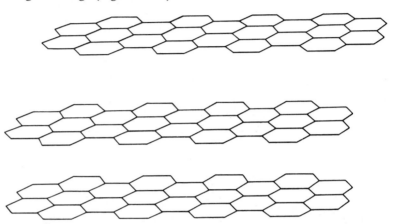

**Figure 4.23**    *The structure of graphite.*

The carbon atoms appear to have a valency of only 3, but the orbitals of each atom are able to overlap in such a way that the fourth outer electron is not localised in a covalent bond but can travel anywhere throughout the sheet of atoms. Like the metals graphite conducts electricity by moving electrons. The sheets of carbon atoms are stacked one on top of another, but there are only weak secondary bonds between them. They readily slide over one another, which is why graphite is so soft. This structure of sliding sheets of atoms explains why graphite is used as a lubricant and why a pencil leaves a mark on paper ("lead pencils" contain graphite, not lead; although both metallic lead and silver have been used for drawing).

*Type 4: Substances with high melting temperatures which conduct electricity only in liquid states*

The ionic bond can give the required properties of type 4 – high melting temperatures and electrical conduction in liquid states only. High melting temperatures imply strong forces between all particles. The electrostatic attraction between + and − ions holds them together to form solid crystals. For electrical conduction the ions themselves must be able to move, there being no free electrons as in metals. Ions can only move if the strong bonding of the crystals is disrupted by melting or by dissolving into water (see Book II).

The structure of ionic crystals reflects an orderly arrangement of ions controlled primarily by their charges, sizes and shapes. Common salt, for example, contains sodium ions ($Na^+$) and chloride ions ($Cl^-$) in equal numbers. They have to be equal to maintain overall charge neutrality; if you look at the periodic table (Figure. 4.5) you will see sodium atoms have one electron to lose and chlorine atoms need one to form a full shell. Figure 4.24 shows the arrangement of ions in the crystal. As you can see, the cations and anions alternate throughout the structure.

**cation:** *positive ion*
**anion:** *negative ion*

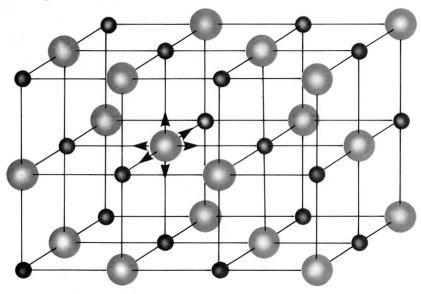

**Figure 4.24** *The structure of sodium chloride. Each positive ion (small) is surrounded by six negative ions (large) as indicated by the arrows, and vice versa.*

The section of crystal illustrated in Figure 4.24 lets you see that each $Cl^-$ ion is surrounded by six $Na^+$ ions. This is the basis of the strong attractive force. The grid of straight lines is only there to show the geometrical arrangement; there are no directional bonds. The electron clouds of the ions would in fact be touching.

You will notice that $Cl^-$ ions are depicted as larger than $Na^+$ ions. It is generally true that cations are small because when electrons have been lost the nucleus holds the remaining cloud a little more tightly than before. Conversely, the extra electrons pushed into anions swell the cloud a little. The larger size of anions, their mutual repulsion and the non-spherical shapes of those which are not single atoms, largely determine the particular arrangements in a crystal. (Lead white, $Pb_2(OH)_2CO_3$, is an example where the anions are of two different kinds and the arrangement of anions and cations is rather complicated.)

**5**

# Relating chemical names to structure

*A*   Forming chemical names

*B*   Inorganic compounds

    *B1*   *The ending -ide*
    *B2*   *The endings -ite and -ate*
    *B3*   *The endings -ous and -ic*
    *B4*   *Salts*

*C*   Organic compounds

    *C1*   *Names derived from those of hydrocarbons*
    *C2*   *Acet- and form- names*
    *C3*   *The modern naming system*
    *C4*   *Benzene derivatives*

# Relating chemical names to structure

Your newly acquired knowledge of bonding can immediately be put to work in understanding the rationale behind systematic chemical names. The major sub-classification is between inorganic (mineral) materials and organic (biological) ones and this chapter aims to show the basis of naming for a reasonable range of each. It cannot be complete but will show you some of the clues by which names come to have meaning.

## *A* Forming chemical names

In everyday language we use slightly different words to carry shades of meaning or to play different grammatical roles in a sentence. (*Conserve, conservator, conservative, conservation.*) The exact construction of each word follows recognised conventions but is really quite arbitrary. *Because* of the conventions we can recognise differences in meaning and function. To understand **chemical names** you have to become similarly sensitive to small differences and be able to interpret them. Thus *sulphuric, sulphurous, sulphide, sulphite* and *sulphate* all obviously have something to do with the element *sulphur*, but each means something slightly different. The problem is that the information is coded and, because the code has been arbitrarily chosen, you just have to learn it.

The main objective behind chemical naming is to describe molecular structure. To do this new names have been created to describe groups of atoms which, although not molecules in their own right, confer recognisable reaction characteristics on a molecule and often remain intact through a reaction. These groups are known as

**radical**      **radicals**. In an exercise you were asked to draw a structure for the organic compound methylamine – the name tells those who know the code that the molecule consists of a methyl group, $CH_3-$, bonded to an amine group, $-NH_2$. It must be $CH_3-NH_2$: the name tells the structure.

Organic chemistry is defined as the chemistry of carbon and its compounds. It deals predominantly with covalent molecules made from a very small range of elements (carbon, hydrogen, oxygen and nitrogen being the most common). Inorganic chemistry is the study of the reactions of all elements other than carbon. A great many inorganic compounds are ionic and so the anions and cations are the radicals used as the basis for the naming systems. Although these names make up quite an extensive vocabulary only a limited selection will be used in this chapter, to show you how small variations in names can imply differences in structure. Often you will find fragments of element names and group names joined with prefixes and suffixes to form new group names, eg *bi-sulphite* compiled from *bi-*, *sulph* and *-ite*. You will be aware of many such names on the bottles in your workshop.

The systems for inorganic and organic naming will be dealt with separately, although they do have something in common which is **suffixes and prefixes**      the use of **suffixes and prefixes** derived from Greek and Latin. Most common are the prefixes telling how many atoms or groups there are in a molecule:

*mono*–one
*di*–two
*tri*–three
*tetra*–four
*penta*–five
*hexa*–six
*hepta*–seven
*octa*–eight
*nona*–nine
*deca*–ten

The compound names *carbon monoxide, monosodium glutamate, carbon disulphide, sulphur trioxide, dinitrogen tetroxide*, give some examples of their use.

# *B* Inorganic compounds

## *Covalent molecules*

Some simple covalent molecules have trivial names which must be learned, as they give no real clue to the elements present or to the way in which they are combined. Water, $H_2O$; ammonia, $NH_3$; and ozone, $O_3$; are examples. Systematic names such as *carbon disulphide*, $CS_2$, and *sulphur dioxide*, $SO_2$, and *dinitrogen tetroxide*, $N_2O_4$, are self-explanatory. More complex inorganic covalent molecules are named using systems related to those described for the organic compounds.

*Ionic compounds*

Calcium hydroxide, lead carbonate, potassium permanganate, sodium bisulphite and copper sulphate are names with which you are probably familiar. Notice that each is a **two-word name**, the first word being the name of a metal. Because you now know that metals form ionic compounds with the metal atoms becoming positive ions, you might correctly deduce that the other part of each name describes a negative ion. Let us look at the way anion names are formed.

**two-word name**

## B1 The ending -IDE

Two negative ions for which you have met electron structures are oxide and chloride. These are the ions formed when an atom of oxygen or of chlorine, acquires enough electrons to fill its outer shell. Oxygen needs two electrons to form $O^{2-}$ and chlorine one electron to form $Cl^-$. These are examples of negative ions formed from a single atom of an element and there are several others:

| | | | |
|---|---|---|---|
| fluoride | $F^-$ | oxide | $O^{2-}$ |
| chloride | $Cl^-$ | sulphide | $S^{2-}$ |
| bromide | $Br^-$ | nitride | $N^{3-}$ |
| iodide | $I^-$ | carbide | $C^{4-}$ |
| hydride | $H^-$ | | |

There are a few anions whose names end in *-ide* which contain atoms of more than one element. Examples of such stable negative ion groups are hydroxide, $OH^-$; and cyanide, $CN^-$.

## B2 The endings -ITE and -ATE

When the ending *-ite* does not occur in a two-part name but is found in a single word name (such as *malachite* or *azurite*), it shows that this is the trivial name for a particular mineral. (Occasionally it denotes other sorts of trivial or trade names such as *dynamite*.)

In compound names the endings *-ite* and *-ate* are commonly found in conjunction with part of an element name. There are examples where both endings occur such as *nitrate* and *nitrite*, *chlorate* and *chlorite*. There are others such as *carbonate* and *silicate* which only occur as *-ates*. All these are names of negative ions formed by oxygen combining with the indicated element:

| | |
|---|---|
| carbonate | $CO_3^{2-}$ |
| phosphate | $PO_4^{3-}$ |
| silicate | $SiO_4^{4-}$ |

The endings *-ite* and *-ate* distinguish between ions containing different amounts of oxygen. An *-ite* ion always contains one less oxygen atom than the corresponding *-ate* ion, and so for the examples mentioned, the formulae for the ions are:

| **-ITE** | | **-ATE** | |
|---|---|---|---|
| nit*rite* | $NO_2^-$ | nit*rate* | $NO_3^-$ |
| sulph*ite* | $SO_3^{2-}$ | sulph*ate* | $SO_4^{2-}$ |
| chlor*ite* | $ClO_2^-$ | chlor*ate* | $ClO_3^-$ |

### Further modification by prefixes

This simple rule is not sufficient as some families of ions have more than two members. Prefixes are used to increase the number of names. They have the following meanings:

*hypo* —containing *less* oxygen than . . .
*per* —containing *more* oxygen than . . .
*thio* —containing a sulphur atom in place of an oxygen
*bi* —containing twice as many anions
*sesqui* —containing $1\frac{1}{2}$ times as many anions.

There are four ions formed by combinations of chlorine and oxygen: $ClO^-$, $ClO_2^-$, $ClO_3^-$, and $ClO_4^-$. The middle of these are already named above, but names are needed for the ion $ClO^-$ containing *less* oxygen than chlorite and for $ClO_4^-$ which contains *more* oxygen than chlorate. Using the relevant prefixes the whole family of names is therefore:

$ClO^-$ hypochlorite

$ClO_2^-$ chlorite

$ClO_3^-$ chlorate

$ClO_4^-$ perchlorate

The prefix *per-* is also met in the peroxide ion, $O_2^{2-}$, which contains more oxygen than the oxide $O^{2-}$. (Hydrogen peroxide, $H_2O_2$, contains more oxygen than water, $H_2O$.) *Per-* is also found in permanganate, $MnO_4^-$, as in potassium permanganate, $KMnO_4$. Since the *per-* compounds contain excess oxygen it is not surprising that they are strong oxidizing agents (see Book II).

In the thiosulphate anion, one oxygen atom in the sulphate ion, $SO_4^{2-}$, has been replaced by a sulphur atom to form $S_2O_3^{2-}$. The prefixes *bi-* and *sesqui-*, although still common, are now archaic. The salt $NaHSO_3$ is now called *sodium hydrogen sulphite* in preference to *sodium bisulphite*. *Bi-* meaning "twice as much", referred to the fact that $NaHSO_3$ contains twice as much $SO_3^{2-}$ per sodium ion as does $Na_2SO_3$, sodium sulphite. Sodium carbonate, $Na_2CO_3$, and sodium bicarbonate, $NaHCO_3$, are similarly related and $Na_3H(CO_3)_2$ is sodium sesquicarbonate, containing one and a half times as much $CO_3^{2-}$ per $Na^+$ ion as the plain carbonate.

**Common examples are**

| | | | |
|---|---|---|---|
| hypochlorite | $ClO^-$ | bicarbonate | $HCO_3^-$ |
| perchlorate | $ClO_4^-$ | bisulphate | $HSO_4^-$ |
| peroxide | $O_2^{2-}$ | bisulphite | $HSO_3^-$ |
| permanganate | $MnO_4^-$ | thiosulphate | $S_2O_3^{2-}$ |

### B3 Words ending in -OUS and -IC

The suffixes *-ous* and *-ic* are found in the first word of two-part names. They usually refer to types of cation, and distinguish different electronic states of a particular metal. The words are not always formed directly from the element name. Many of the metals that have been in common use for a long time do not have names ending in -um or -ium, whereas most of the other metal elements do. Where the common name is difficult to use in this way, the -*ous* and -*ic* words are formed from the Latin name for the metal.

| Metal | Latin name | Symbol |
|-------|-----------|--------|
| copper | cuprum | Cu |
| gold | aurum | Au |
| iron | ferrum | Fe |
| lead | plumbum | Pb |
| silver | argentum | Ag |
| tin | stannum | Sn |

An example you may well have met concerns the corrosion of copper. Copper forms two oxides, a dull red substance, $Cu_2O$, and a black substance, $CuO$. Since oxygen needs two electrons to achieve a full electron shell you can see that in $Cu_2O$ each copper atom is giving one electron while the one copper atom in $CuO$ give two electrons. The names of these compounds are *cuprous oxide* for $Cu_2O$ and *cupric oxide* for $CuO$. The suffix to use in the lower valency state is -*ous* and in the higher valency state, -*ic*. In the -*ic* condition an atom has given away more of its electrons than in the -*ous* state.

The following exercise will help to familiarise you with the names. Underline the appropriate description of each of the given compounds before checking your answer by reading on. The charges on the anions were given in previous sections.

| | | | | |
|---|---|---|---|---|
| **a** | copper sulphate | $CuSO_4$ | cuprous | cupric |
| **b** | iron oxide | $FeO$ | ferrous | ferric |
| **c** | iron oxide | $Fe_2O_3$ | ferrous | ferric |
| **d** | tin chloride | $SnCl_4$ | stannous | stannic |
| **e** | lead carbonate | $PbCO_3$ | plumbous | plumbic |

The valencies or possible valencies of the positive and negative ions in the examples are:

| Positive | | Negative | |
|----------|---|----------|---|
| $Cu^+$ | 1 valent | $SO_4^{2-}$ | 2 valent |
| $Cu^{2+}$ | 2 valent | $O^{2-}$ | 2 valent |
| $Fe^{2+}$ | 2 valent | $Cl^-$ | 1 valent |
| $Fe^{3+}$ | 3 valent | $CO_3^{2-}$ | 2 valent |
| $Sn^{2+}$ | 2 valent | | |
| $Sn^{4+}$ | 4 valent | | |
| $Pb^{2+}$ | 2 valent | | |
| $Pb^{4+}$ | 4 valent | | |

The formula shows the numbers of ions which balance one another electrically. Thus in (a) one copper ion is associated with one sulphate ion. The latter is charged 2 − so the copper ion must have given two electrons and be 2 + which is cup*ic*.

By this line of reasoning you find that the ions are:

**a** cupric     $Cu^{2+}$
**b** ferrous    $Fe^{2+}$
**c** ferric*    $Fe^{3+}$     * $(3 \times (-2)$ is the total charge for oxygen,
**d** stannic    $Sn^{4+}$     therefore $2 \times (+3)$ is the total charge for iron.)
**e** plumbous   $Pb^{2+}$

**acids**

You also meet -ous and -ic words when describing **acids**. You can regard **acids** as combinations of hydrogen with negative ions. The reason for regarding them as special is that when the acid is pure the negative part is forced to make a *covalent* bond with the hydrogen. Thus $H_2SO_4$, sulphuric acid, is a true molecule while $CuSO_4$ is a part of a crystal. Another name is needed for the molecule $H_2SO_3$ to distinguish it from sulphur*ic* acid; it is sulphur*ous* acid.

### B4  Salts

The combinations of metal ions and negative ions from acids are collectively known as *salts*. "Common salt", sodium chloride, is just one example. It is instructive to see how it is formed in a reaction between hydrochloric acid and sodium hydroxide. When in solution in water, hydrochloric acid, HCl, breaks to form the ions $H^+$ and $Cl^-$ while sodium hydroxide, NaOH, dissolves to give $Na^+$ and $OH^-$ ions, producing a mixture of $Na^+$, $Cl^-$, $H^+$ and $OH^-$. Almost all the $H^+$ and $OH^-$ ions join up to form *covalently* bonded water molecules, $H_2O$, leaving $Na^+$ and $Cl^-$ only. If the solution dries out these ions cohere electrostatically to form crystals of salt.

Acids whose name is of the form *hydro...ic* react to give salts which end in *-ide*; hydrobromic acid produces bromides. Acids whose names are formed simply from the element name plus *-ic* give rise to *-ate* salts; phosphoric acid produces phosphates. Acids ending in *-ous* produce *-ite* salts; sulphurous acid gives sulphites.

The cationic part of a salt is not always a metal. Ammonia, $NH_3$, reacts with acids to form salts containing the cation $NH_4^+$. This is called the *ammonium* ion, the *-ium* ending showing that it forms salts like a metal, such as sodium.

# C  Organic compounds

Organic compounds may contain large numbers of atoms of only a few elements. There are 35 possible structures for the molecule $C_9H_{20}$, which contains 29 atoms and only two different elements. Obviously, a naming system which uses only the element name as a root with a few prefixes and suffixes is not sufficient. Several ways of overcoming this difficulty have been attempted.

Before molecular structure was understood, compounds were often named after their source; formic acid was extracted from ants, and acetic acid from vinegar. The names are formed from the Latin words for "ant" and "vinegar". These are trivial names (see Chapter 2) which identify specifically but do not indicate structure. When a new compound was made by a reaction of, say, acetic acid, the new product would be given the prefix acet- and an ending to show what sort of change had taken place. This introduces the idea of a group or part of a molecule which remains intact throughout the reaction. Other groups which remain unchanged in a reaction are those derived from hydrocarbons, like ethyl and methyl from ethane and methane. A naming system has been devised which is based on these hydrocarbon names. The most modern system works by looking at all carbon compounds as a backbone of carbon atoms with various radicals attached to it. By using numbers you can designate which carbon atom each radical is attached to.

Although they are very precise, the newer naming systems can be very cumbersome and have not been universally accepted. The result is that for common substances trivial, old system and new system names are used side by side. Thus you find that acetone, dimethyl ketone and propan-2-one are the same compound. Consequently we have to discuss all three systems in this book.

## C1 Names derived from those of hydrocarbons

The simplest organic molecules are the **hydrocarbons**, made of carbon and hydrogen alone. They are most commonly met as fuels (petrol, diesel oil, natural gas) which are mixtures of several different molecules. One hydrocarbon mixture commonly used in conservation is white spirit. Occasionally benzene, toluene and xylene are used as solvents, even though they are toxic.

**hydrocarbons**

You need to learn the names and structures of some simple hydrocarbons, as the names of radicals containing only C and H atoms such as methyl- and ethyl- are derived from them. You are already familiar with methane, $CH_4$. This is the smallest hydrocarbon molecule and has just one carbon atom. The names and structures of some other hydrocarbons are given below.

| Number of carbon atoms | Formula | Name | Structure |
|---|---|---|---|
| 1 | $CH_4$ | methane | H—C—H (with H above and H below) |
| 2 | $C_2H_6$ | ethane | H—C—C—H (with H above and below each C) |
| 3 | $C_3H_8$ | propane | H—C—C—C—H (with H above and below each C) |
| 4 | $C_4H_{10}$ | butane | H—C—C—C—C—H (with H above and below each C) |

When more than four carbon atoms are joined in a line the names correspond to Greek numbers:

five carbons gives pentane: $C_5H_{12}$
six carbons gives hexane: $C_6H_{14}$
seven carbons gives heptane: $C_7H_{16}$
eight carbons gives octane: $C_8H_{18}$
nine carbons gives nonane: $C_9H_{20}$

If one of the hydrogen atoms comes off the end of such a hydrocarbon molecule, a radical which can join on to something else will be formed. The free bond is denoted by an unattached dash:

| Number of carbon atoms | Name | Formula |
| --- | --- | --- |
| 1 | methyl | $CH_3-$ |
| 2 | ethyl | $C_2H_5-$ |
| 3 | propyl | $C_3H_7-$ |
| 4 | butyl | $C_4H_9-$ |
| 5 | pentyl | $C_5H_{11}-$ |

(The pentyl group was formerly known as *amyl*.)

**alkyl radicals** As a class these groups are called the **alkyl radicals**. If, in a formula, an unspecified alkyl group is to be shown it is usually represented by the letter R—.

In the parent hydrocarbons, as the molecular chain gets longer different physical properties are manifested and the following trend is shown:

| Number of carbon atoms | Physical state | Name | Uses |
| --- | --- | --- | --- |
| 1 to 4 | gas | natural gas | gas fuels |
| 7 to 9 | volatile, mobile liquid | petrol (gasoline) | car fuel |
| 10 to 12 | less volatile, less mobile liquid | paraffin (kerosene) | jet engine fuel |
| 13 to 18 | sluggish liquid | diesel oil | heavy engine fuel |
| 20s | slimy liquid | oil | lubrication |
| several tens | soft solid | wax | candles |
| several hundreds | stiffer solid | polythene | plastic |

This trend is followed to some extent by compounds containing the groups with the same numbers of carbon atoms. So the name begins to tell you something about the physical properties of the compound.

The group to which the alkyl group R— is attached is what dictates the chemical behaviour of the compound. The reactive groups of **functional group** atoms are called **functional groups**. An example is the —OH group. This is the functional group in the class of compounds **alcohols** R—OH which are known as the **alcohols**. The name of a specific compound is formed by adding the name of the alkyl group to the class name. Thus $C_2H_5-$ (ethyl) joined to $-OH$ (alcohol) makes $C_2H_5OH$, ethyl alcohol.

Figure 5.1 lists some functional groups and the names of the classes of compounds in which they are found.

| Class name | Functional group | Typical structure* | Example |
|---|---|---|---|
| alcohol | $-OH$ | $R-OH$ | $C_2H_5OH$ ethyl alcohol |
| amine | $-NH_2$ | $R-NH_2$ | $CH_3NH_2$ methylamine |
| alkyl halide | $-F$ $-Cl$ $-Br$ $-I$ | $R-F$ $R-Cl$ $R-Br$ $R-I$ | $CH_3Br$ methyl bromide |
| ether | $-O-$ | $R-O-R'$ | $C_2H_5OC_2H_5$ diethyl ether |
| ketone | $\overset{O}{\overset{\|\|}{-C-}}$ | $\overset{O}{\overset{\|\|}{R-C-R'}}$ | $CH_3-CO-C_2H_5$ methyl ethyl ketone |

\* *R and R' are alkyl radicals, not necessarily identical.*

**Figure 5.1**

Using this chart you should be able to give names to the compounds whose formulae are shown here:

| formula | name |
|---|---|
| **a** $CH_3OH$ | |
| **b** $C_3H_7OH$ | |
| **c** $C_2H_5NH_2$ | |
| **d** $CH_3OCH_3$ | |

You should have written (a) methyl alcohol, (b) propyl alcohol, (c) ethylamine, (d) dimethyl ether.

## *Other radicals*

Propane, $C_3H_8$, has two different types of hydrogen atom, those on the end carbon atoms and those on the central one. If a hydrogen

**prefixes n- and iso-** atom from one of the end carbons is lost the *normal propyl* (or n-propyl) radical is formed, $CH_3CH_2CH_2-$. If a hydrogen atom from the central atom is lost the *isopropyl* radical results

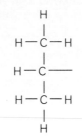

isopropyl alcohol (IPA) is a common solvent in conservation workshops.

Another hydrocarbon-derived radical whose name you will be **vinyl** familiar with is the **vinyl** group.

It is derived from ethylene. Combined with −OH it becomes vinyl alcohol and with −Cl, vinyl chloride. These names are used with the prefix *poly-*, which means many, to describe the compounds polyvinyl alcohol and polyvinyl chloride (PVC), used as adhesives and plastic sheeting. **Polymerization**, the joining together of units such as vinyl alcohol into long molecular chains, will be discussed in full in Book III.

## C2 The ACET- and FORM- names

Acetone and formaldehyde are organic chemicals you will know. Formic acid has been used to clean corroded silver and acetic acid to fix fugitive dyes before washing textiles. Their names are examples of the class of compounds beginning with *form-* and *acet-*. All the *form-* compounds contain the group of atoms

and all the *acet-* compounds contain the group

The name of the compound depends on what other atom or group of atoms is attached to the free bond. The names and structures of some of these compounds are given in Figure 5.2.

| Group added | Form- | | Acet- | | Class name |
|---|---|---|---|---|---|
| | **Names** | **Structure** | **Names** | **Structure** | |
| H | formaldehyde | $H-C{\overset{O}{\underset{H}{}}}$ | acetaldehyde | $CH_3-C{\overset{O}{\underset{H}{}}}$ | aldehyde |
| OH | formic acid | $H-C{\overset{O}{\underset{OH}{}}}$ | acetic acid | $CH_3-C{\overset{O}{\underset{OH}{}}}$ | acid |
| $NH_2$ | formamide | $H-C{\overset{O}{\underset{NH_2}{}}}$ | acetamide | $CH_3-C{\overset{O}{\underset{NH_2}{}}}$ | amide |
| $O-C_2H_5$ | ethyl formate | $H-C{\overset{O}{\underset{O-C_2H_5}{}}}$ | ethyl acetate | $CH_3-C{\overset{O}{\underset{O-C_2H_5}{}}}$ | ester |
| ONa | sodium formate | $H-C{\overset{O}{\underset{O^-Na^+}{}}}$ | sodium acetate | $CH_3-C{\overset{O}{\underset{O^-Na^+}{}}}$ | salt |
| $CH_3$ | — | — | acetone | $CH_3-C{\overset{O}{\underset{CH_3}{}}}$ | ketone |

**Figure 5.2**

These groups of names use a stem which comes from the trivial name for the organic acids. Some other acids give rise to compounds whose names are formed in the same way and whose names may be familiar. The class of compounds called aldehydes are all named in this fashion, eg

$$\text{propionaldehyde } C_2H_5-\overset{\overset{\textstyle O}{\|}}{C}-H \text{ from propionic acid } C_2H_5-\overset{\overset{\textstyle O}{\|}}{C}-OH$$

$$\text{butyraldehyde } C_3H_7-\overset{\overset{\textstyle O}{\|}}{C}-H \text{ from butyric acid } C_3H_7-\overset{\overset{\textstyle O}{\|}}{C}-OH$$

The acids, whose names all end in *-ic*, can form salts whose names all end in *-ate*.

Palmitic acid $C_{15}H_{31}COOH$ and

Stearic acid $C_{17}H_{35}COOH$

form palmitates and stearates which are found in soap.

**Organic acids** also react with alcohols to form a class of compounds called **esters**. You might like to imagine these as the organic

**organic acids**

**esters**

equivalent of salts as there is some similarity between the reaction shown below and that described in section B4.

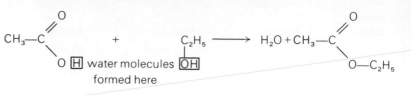

Acetic acid plus ethyl alcohol forms ethyl acetate plus water.

These reactions are usually very slow but can be important. They account to some extent for the changes in fine wines as they mature, esters giving bouquet and delicate flavour replacing the sharpness of acids present in the young wines. Vinyl acetate

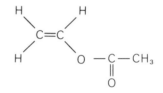

is the basic unit of the familiar PVA group of adhesives.

## C3 The modern naming system

The first attempts at a system of naming which indicated molecular structure failed largely because too many starting-points were used. We have looked at two of them – the names based on hydrocarbon names and those using the early names for natural acids. With hindsight, another reason is that organic chemists came to make and analyse the structure of so many complicated molecules that a system built on pairs of radical names simply could not cope.

The key to the new system is to count the number of carbon atoms linked together in a chain. The appropriate fragment of the hydrocarbon name then forms a basis for the compound name depending on what bits are attached. A code is used to describe groups substituted for hydrogen. You will notice some connections with the earlier names.

$-OH$     gives an ending -*ol*

$-CHO$    gives an ending -*al*

$-C = O$ gives an ending -*one*

$- COOH$ gives an encoding -*oic acid*

(The carbon atoms in the last three are counted as part of the hydrocarbon fragment)

Thus there are those regarded as derived from methane

These are:

| New systematic names | | Old systematic names |
|---|---|---|

methanol

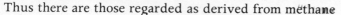

methyl alcohol

methanal        H—C = O        formaldehyde

methanoic acid        H—O—C = O        formic acid

and with two carbon atoms:

ethane

ethanol        ethyl alcohol

ethanal        acetaldehyde

ethanoic acid        acetic acid

Three carbon atom chain molecules have their names based on propane ($CH_3CH_2CH_3$) as follows:

| New name | | Old name |
|---|---|---|
| propan – 1 – ol | $CH_3CH_2CH_2OH$ | n-propyl alcohol |
| propan – 2 – ol | $CH_3CH(OH)CH_3$ | isopropyl alcohol |
| propanal | $CH_3CH_2CHO$ | propionaldehyde |
| propan – 2 – one | $CH_3COCH_3$ | acetone |

The numbers indicate the carbon atom to which the functional group is attached. So, in propan – 2 – ol, the OH is attached to the second C as you read the molecular formula. Here you can begin to see the strength of the system but also its clumsiness in speech.

In some compounds the carbon chain is interrupted by an atom of a different element, as in ethers and esters. The substance with the old systematic name of ethyl acetate has the structure:

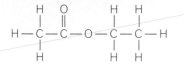

It is an ester of ethanoic acid and is now called ethyl ethanoate.

**ethers**　　Ethers are regarded as substituted hydrocarbons. Thus diethyl ether (commonly just called "ether") is thought of as ethane with one H replaced by an ethoxy ($C_2H_5 - O -$) group and so $C_2H_5 - O - C_2H_5$ becomes ethoxyethane:

(H) is removed                    and substituted by

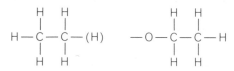

This new system of naming will not be pursued further here, although it is hoped that you can now see that it contains rules which are well enough defined to express very complicated structures – and this is precisely its function. Except in simple cases (such as ethanol) the new systematic names do, if anything, encourage the use of trivial names in casual scientific conversation.

---

*Exercise*

1　Deduce the structures of the following substances:

　　**a** 1.2. dichloroethane　　　　　(ethylene chloride)
　　**b** 1. 1. 1. trichloroethane　　　　(methyl chloroform)
　　**c** 2-ethoxyethanol　　　　　　　(cellosolve)
　　**d** 1-pentyl, 1-ethanoate　　　　　(amyl acetate)
　　**e** NN-dimethyl amino methanal　　(dimethyl formamide)

*Note*: the NN symbol in **e** means that there are two groups attached to the nitrogen atom, and the three number ones in **b** mean that there are three substituted H atoms on one carbon atom.

## C4 Benzene derivatives

All the organic compounds described so far have been formed from straight chains of carbon atoms. There is also an important group of chemicals in which the carbon atoms are joined together in a ring.

**-ane**　　The name-ending **-ane** is used for hydrocarbons which contain
**-ene**　　only single bonds (methane, butane). The suffix **-ene** refers to hydrocarbons with double bonds in their structure (ethylene, now called ethene). The ending *-ene* also occurs in the hydrocarbons benzene, toluene and xylene which have all been used as solvents in conservation work despite their toxicity.

Benzene, $C_6H_6$, has a molecule with a **ring** of 6 carbon atoms and originally, to fit with the idea of carbon having a valency of 4 the structure of Figure 5.3 was proposed

**ring compounds**

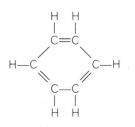

**Figure 5.3** *Old idea for the structure of benzene.*

You can see that the double bonds in the ring could justify the -ene ending on the name. However, the rings do not show the chemical reactions typical of double bonds. With the advent of ideas concerning molecular orbitals came a realisation that the carbon ring is made of single covalent bonds with the remaining six electrons in orbitals joining all six carbon atoms. Thus all the electrons are equally shared. These rings are very stable and occur in a host of compounds (collectively known as *aromatic* compounds). As it is such a common structural element, a symbol, ⬡ , is now frequently used. The hexagon indicates the single bonds and the circle denotes the six electrons circulating around the ring. Notice that even the atom symbols have gone; a C – H is assumed at each corner of the hexagon.

Toluene $C_7H_8$ can be thought of as derived from benzene by the substitution of a methyl group ($CH_3-$) for one of the hydrogen atoms; so its structure is:

that is, $C_6H_5 - CH_3$, since one of the hydrogens of ⬡ has been dropped to make room for the methyl group. Xylene has two such substitutions and can therefore exist as three isomers. Commercial xylene is a mixture of all three types.

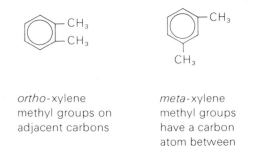

*ortho*-xylene
methyl groups on
adjacent carbons

*meta*-xylene
methyl groups
have a carbon
atom between
them

*para*-xylene
methyl groups on
opposite corners
of hexagon

**Figure 5.4** *Structures for xylene.*

The prefix *para* will be familiar from the name of the insecticide para-dichlorobenzene:

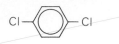

In the modern naming system the carbon atoms in the ring are numbered. The three possible isomers of xylene become 1.2.dimethyl benzene, 1.3.dimethyl benzene and 1.4.dimethyl benzene.

**phenyl**    The radical $C_6H_5-$ is called the **phenyl** group, so toluene could be called phenyl methane (or methyl benzene). Most of the benzene derivatives are more commonly known by their trivial names.

Phenyl amine or amino benzene, 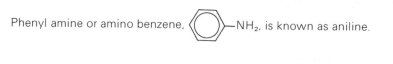 $-NH_2$, is known as aniline.

Phenyl alcohol or hydroxy benzene, $-OH$ is known as phenol.

Phenyl ethylene or vinyl benzene, is called styrene, which is the basic unit of the polymer polystyrene.

## Conclusion

You should by now have a grasp of the theory of basic chemistry. In the next book in the series, which deals with the scientific aspects of cleaning, you will start to use the theory in practice. The dirt on an object is frequently chemically very complex, and it is held on to the object by secondary bonds, which are related to the primary the bonding mechanisms discussed in this book. The theory you have learnt should enable you to make an informed choice between the many available methods to break the bonds without damaging the object you are working on.

# Answers

## Chapter 3

1  **a**  One atom of carbon     C
      two atoms of oxygen   $O_2$
   **b**  two atoms of hydrogen $H_2$
      one atom of sulphur    S
      four atoms of oxygen   $O_4$
   **c**  three atoms of carbon  $C_3$
      six atoms of hydrogen  $H_6$
      one atom of oxygen    O

2  **a**  $H_2O$;     **b**  $NH_3$;     **c**  $C_6H_6$

3  **a**  $C_3H_8 + 5O_2 \rightarrow 3CO_2 + 4H_2O$
   **b**  $2C_4H_{10} + 13O_2 \rightarrow 8CO_2 + 10H_2O$

4
$$CaCO_3 \xrightarrow{\text{heat}} CaO + CO_2$$
calcium carbonate $\longrightarrow$ calcium oxide + carbon dioxide

5
$$CaCO_3 + H_2SO_4 \longrightarrow CaSO_4 + H_2O + CO_2$$

calcium carbonate + sulphuric acid $\longrightarrow$ calcium sulphate + water + carbon dioxide

6  Carbon dioxide.

7  The molecular formulae are  **a**  $CH_4$ for methane;
                                     **b**  $O_2$ for oxygen;
                                     **c**  $H_2O$ for water.
   The molecular weights are therefore:
   Methane, $CH_4$ = (1 × 12)       + (4 × 1)
                   (one carbon)  + (four hydrogens)
                = 16

   Oxygen, $O_2$    = 2 × 16
                   (two oxygens)
                = 32

   Water, $H_2O$    = (2 × 1)       + (1 × 16)
                   (two hydrogens) + (one oxygen)
                = 18

## Chapter 4

1  Check answer against the table above.
2  To enable each atom to make its correct number of links, the answers must be:

   **a**  $H_2$ is H – H
   **b**  $N_2$ is N ≡ N

   **c**  ammonia is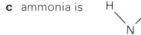

   **d**  methylamine is

   **e**  vinyl chloride contains a double bond thus

   **f**

This is vinyl alcohol, the basic unit of polyvinyl alcohol.

3  Nitrogen atoms have five electrons outside the helium (two-electron) shell. To become like neon each atom must acquire a share in three more electrons. So the structures are as:

   **a**  Ammonia $NH_3$                      **b**  Nitrogen $N_2$

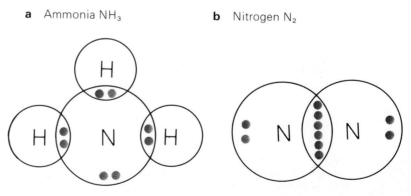

**c**  Methylamine $CH_3 - NH_2$

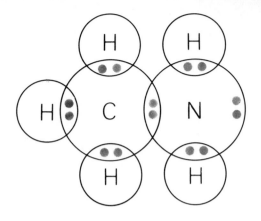

# Chapter 5

1 **a**

```
      Cl  Cl
      |   |
  H — C — C — H
      |   |
      H   H
```

That the Cls are on different C atoms is shown by the prefix 1, 2.

**b**

```
      Cl  H
      |   |
  Cl— C — C — H
      |   |
      Cl  H
```

1, 1, 1 tells you that all the Cls are on the same C atom.

**c**  $C_2H_5 — O — CH_2 — CH_2OH$
Ethanol $C_2H_5OH$ has had an H on the C atom which is not carrying OH
substituted by ethoxy $C_2H_5O-$

**d**

$$CH_3 — C \overset{\displaystyle O}{\underset{\displaystyle O—C_5H_{11}}{\Large\|}}$$

Ethanoate is the same as acetate. Here the H of the OH in ethanoic acid
has been substituted by the pentyl chain.

**e**

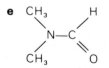

Methanal is HCHO; aminomethanal has an H replaced by $NH_2$ to
become $NH_2CHO$. Now the Hs of the amino group have been replaced
by $CH_3-$ groups.

# Full periodic table of elements

*number of electrons in outer shell*

| | 1 | 2 | | | | | | | | | | | 3 | 4 | 5 | 6 | 7 | 8 |
|---|---|---|---|---|---|---|---|---|---|---|---|---|---|---|---|---|---|---|
| period 1 | 1 H 1 | | | | | | | | | | | | | | | | | 2 He 4 |
| period 2 | 3 Li 7 | 4 Be 9 | | | | | | | | | | | 5 B 11 | 6 C 12 | 7 N 14 | 8 O 16 | 9 F 19 | 10 Ne 20 |
| period 3 | 11 Na 23 | 12 Mg 24 | | | | | | | | | | | 13 Al 27 | 14 Si 28 | 15 P 31 | 16 S 32 | 17 Cl 35 | 18 A 40 |
| period 4 | 19 K 39 | 20 Ca 40 | 21 Sc 45 | 22 Ti 48 | 23 V 51 | 24 Cr 52 | 25 Mn 55 | 26 Fe 56 | 27 Co 59 | 28 Ni 59 | 29 Cu 64 | 30 Zn 65 | 31 Ga 70 | 32 Ge 73 | 33 As 75 | 34 Se 79 | 35 Br 80 | 36 Kr 84 |
| period 5 | 37 Rb 85 | 38 Sr 88 | 39 Y 89 | 40 Zr 91 | 41 Nb 93 | 42 Mo 96 | 43 Tc 98 | 44 Ru 101 | 45 Rh 103 | 46 Pd 106 | 47 Ag 108 | 48 Cd 112 | 49 In 115 | 50 Sn 119 | 51 Sb 122 | 52 Te 128 | 53 I 127 | 54 Xe 131 |
| period 6 | 55 Cs 133 | 56 Ba 137 | 57* La 139 | 72 Hf 178 | 73 Ta 181 | 74 W 184 | 75 Re 186 | 76 Os 190 | 77 Ir 192 | 78 Pt 195 | 79 Au 197 | 80 Hg 201 | 81 Tl 204 | 82 Pb 207 | 83 Bi 209 | 84 Po 210 | 85 At 210 | 86 Rn 222 |
| period 7 | 87 Fr 223 | 88 Ra 226 | 89† Ac 227 | | | | | | | | | | | | | | | |

* Lanthanides (so-called for the names of the first element in the series)

| 57 La 139 | 58 Ce 140 | 59 Pr 141 | 60 Nd 144 | 61 Pm 147 | 62 Sm 150 | 63 Eu 152 | 64 Gd 157 | 65 Tb 159 | 66 Dy 162 | 67 Ho 165 | 68 Er 167 | 69 Tm 169 | 70 Yb 173 | 71 Lu 175 |
|---|---|---|---|---|---|---|---|---|---|---|---|---|---|---|

† Actinides (so-called for the names of the first element in the series)

| 89 Ac 227 | 90 Th 232 | 91 Pa 231 | 92 U 238 | 93 Np 237 | 94 Pu 242 | 95 Am 243 | 96 Cm 247 | 97 Bk 247 | 98 Cf 251 | 99 Es 254 | 100 Fm 253 | 101 Md 256 | 102 No 254 | 103 Lw 257 |
|---|---|---|---|---|---|---|---|---|---|---|---|---|---|---|

The number printed above the symbol for each element is its atomic number; the number below is its relative atomic mass

# Recommended reading

Conservation science is a comparatively young discipline which has yet to develop a distinctive literature of its own. There are relatively few dedicated textbooks, and most advances in knowledge and techniques are to be found in conference preprints and proceedings and in journal articles. One consequence is that conservation students, perhaps more than others, have to ferret out the literature they require. Another is that it is not possible to present here a bibliography which precisely matches the material in this book, topic by topic.

Listed below is a selection of English language works from conservation and other disciplines which are likely to be most rewarding. They should be available in any well-equipped conservation library. The individual papers contained within them, in the journals listed and indeed in the wider international conservation literature, can be located with the help of Art and Archaeology Technical Abstracts and/or on-line via the Conservation Information Network. The latter also offers a materials database which provides technical data on conservation materials, using many of the concepts explained in this book.

## International Institute for Conservation (IIC) Publications

*Congress preprints:*

Preprints for the IIC Rome Conference 1961 (bound volume of conference papers distributed to delegates); published as *Recent Advances in Conservation*, edited by G. Thomson, Butterworth, London, 1963.

Preprints for the IIC Delft Conference 1964 (bound volume of conference papers distributed to delegates); a fuller version in similar format appeared as *IIC 1964 Delft Conference on the Conservation of Textiles Collected Preprints*, 2nd edition, IIC, London, 1965; published as *Textile Conservation*, edited by Jentina E. Leene, Butterworth, London, 1972.

Preprints for the contributions to the London Conference on *Museum Climatology*, edited by Garry Thomson, IIC, London, 1967; revised edition May 1968.

Preprints for the contributions to the New York Conference on *Conservation of Stone and Wooden Objects*, IIC, London, 1970; second edition, edited by

Garry Thomson, published in two volumes, Volume 1 *Stone*, Volume 2 *Wooden Objects*, August 1972; subsequently reprinted as a single volume.

*Conservation of Paintings and the Graphic Arts*, preprints for the contributions to the Lisbon Congress 1972, IIC, London, 1972; published as *Conservation and Restoration of Pictorial Art*, edited by Norman Brommelle and Perry Smith, Butterworth, London, 1976.

*Conservation in Archaeology and the Applied Arts*, preprints for the contributions to the Stockholm Congress 1975, IIC, London, 1975.

*Conservation of Wood in Painting and the Decorative Arts*, preprints for the contributions to the Oxford Congress, edited by N. S. Brommelle, Anne Moncrieff and Perry Smith, IIC, London, 1978.

*Conservation Within Historic Buildings*, preprints for the contributions to the Vienna Congress, edited by N. S. Brommelle, Garry Thomson and Perry Smith, IIC, London, 1980.

*Science and Technology in the Service of Conservation*, preprints for the contributions to the Washington Congress, edited by N. S. Brommelle and Garry Thomson, IIC, London, 1982.

*Adhesives and Consolidants*, preprints for the contributions to the Paris Congress, edited by N. S. Brommelle, Elizabeth M. Pye, Perry Smith and Garry Thomson, IIC, London, 1984.

*Adhésifs et Consolidants*, Edition française des communications, IIC Xe Congrès International, publiée par la Section Française de l'IIC, Champs-sur-Marne, 1984.

*Case Studies in the Conservation of Stone and Wall Paintings*, preprints for the contributions to the Bologna Congress, edited by N. S. Brommelle and Perry Smith, IIC, London, 1986.

*The Conservation of Far Eastern Art*, preprints for the contributions to the Kyoto Congress, edited by John S. Mills, Perry Smith and Kazuo Yamasaki, IIC, London, 1988.

*Conservation of Far Eastern Art*, abstracts of the contributions to the Kyoto Congress, edited by H. Mabuchi and Perry Smith, Japanese Organizing Committee of the IIC Kyoto Congress, Tokyo, 1968.

*Cleaning, Retouching and Coatings: Technology and Practice for Easel Paintings and Polychrome Sculpture*, preprints for the contributions to the Brussels Congress, edited by John S. Mills and Perry Smith, IIC, London, 1990.

*Cleaning, Retouching and Coatings*, summaries of the posters at the Brussels Congress, IIC, London, 1990.

*Conservation of the Iberian and Latin American Cultural Heritage*, preprints for the contributions to the Madrid Congress, edited by H. W. M. Hodges, John S. Mills and Perry Smith, IIC, London, 1992. An abstracts booklet and a Spanish translation of the preprint volume are also planned.

## ICOM Committee for Conservation

Proceedings of the following triennial meetings: (1966, 1969 and 1972 were not issued as preprints or subsequently published)

4th Triennial Meeting, Venice — 1975.

5th Triennial Meeting, Zagreb — 1978.

6th Triennial Meeting, Ottawa — 1981.

7th Triennial Meeting, Copenhagen — 1984, Diana de Froment (ed.), Paris: ICOM and the J. Paul Getty Trust.

8th Triennial Meeting, Sydney — 1987, Kirsten Grimstad (ed.), Los Angeles: ICOM CC and the Getty Conservation Institute.

9th Triennial Meeting, Dresden — 1990, J. Cliff McCawley (ed.), Los Angeles: ICOM and the Getty Conservation Institute.

## United Kingdom Institute for Conservation (UKIC) Publications

*Occasional Papers Series:*

No. 1  *Conservation, Archaeology and Museums* (1980).

No. 2  *Microscopy in Archaeological Conservation* (1980).

No. 3  *Lead and Tin: Studies in Conservation and Technology* (1982).

No. 4  *Corrosion Inhibitors in Conservation* (1985).

No. 5  *Archaeological Bone, Antler and Ivory* (1987).

No. 6  *Restoration of Early Musical Instruments* (1987).

No. 7  *From Pinheads to Hanging Bowls: The Identification, Deterioration and Conservation of Applied Enamel and Glass Decoration on Archaeological Artifacts* (1987).

No. 8  *Evidence Preserved in Corrosion Products* (1989).

No. 9  *Conservation of Stained Glass* (1989).

No. 10 *Archaeological Textiles* (1990).

Fairbrass, S. and J. Hermans (eds) (1989) *Modern Art: The Restoration and Techniques of Modern Paper and Paints*, London: UKIC.

Hackney, S., J. Townsend and N. Easthaugh (eds) (1990) *Dirt and Pictures Separated*, London: UKIC.

Todd, V. (ed.) (1988) *Conservation Today*, preprints for the 30th Anniversary Conference of UKIC held in October 1988, London: UKIC.

## ICCROM Publications

Masschelein-Kleiner, L. (1985) *Ancient Binding Media, Varnishes and Adhesives*, Rome: ICCROM.

Torraca, G. (1963) *Synthetic Materials used in the Conservation of Cultural Property* (4th edn 1990), Rome: ICCROM.

Torraca, G. (1975) *Solubility and Solvents for Conservation Problems* (3rd edn 1984), Rome: ICCROM.

Torraca, G. (1981) *Porous Building Materials: Materials Science for Architectural Conservation* (3rd rev. edn 1988), Rome: ICCROM.

## Safety literature

Bretherick, L. (ed.) (1986) *Hazards in the Chemical Laboratory,* 4th edn, London: Royal Society of Chemistry.

Clydesdale, A. (1982) *Chemicals in Conservation: A Guide to Possible Hazards and Safe Use* (2nd edn 1987), Edinburgh: Conservation Bureau (Scottish Development Agency) and Scottish Society for Conservation and Restoration.

Howie, F. (ed.) (1987) *Safety in Museums and Galleries,* London: Butterworth with the International Journal of Museum Management.

The Health and Safety Commission (HSC) and the Health and Safety Executive publish a great deal of information which is of interest to conservators. This includes:

> HSE Guidance Notes Series
> Health and Safety (Guidance) Series
> Health and Safety (Regulations) Series.

Many are available free of charge from the HSE. Contact HSE Publications Point, St Hugh's House, Stanley Precinct, Bootle, Merseyside L20 3LZ

A full list of current HSC/E publications "Publications in Series" is published twice yearly and is available from HSE Public Enquiry Points:

Baynards House
1 Chepstow Place
Westbourne Grove
London W2 4TF

Broad Lane
Sheffield S3 7HQ

(This list applies to the UK; most other countries have their own safety organisation.)

## Other books

Allsopp, Dennis and K. J. Seal (1986) *Introduction to Biodeterioration,* London: Edward Arnold.

Black, J. (ed.) (1987) *Recent Advances in the Conservation and Analysis of Artifacts,* Proceedings of the Jubilee Conservation Conference of the University of London Institute of Archaeology, London: Summer Schools Press.

Brill, T. (1980) *Light: Its Interaction with Art and Antiques,* New York: Plenum Press.

Brown, B. F., H. C. Burnett, W. T. Chase, M. Goodway, J. Kruger and M. Pourbaix (eds) (1977) *Corrosion and Metal Artifacts – a Dialogue between Conservators, Archaeologists and Corrosion Scientists,* National Bureau of Standards Special Publication 479, Washington: US Department of Commerce.

Brydson, J. A. (1989) *Plastics Materials* (5th edn), London: Butterworth.

Burns, R. M. and W. W. Bradley (1962) *Protective Coatings for Metals* (3rd edn 1967), New York: Reinhold.

Cotterill, R. (1985) *The Cambridge Guide to the Material World*, Cambridge: Cambridge University Press.

Dana, E. S. (1991) *A Textbook of Mineralogy* (5th edn), New York: Wiley.

Eaton, L. and C. Meredith (eds) (1988) *Modern Organic Materials*, preprints for meeting held in Edinburgh, April 1988, Edinburgh: Scottish Society for Conservation and Restoration.

Feller, R. L. (1986) *Artists' Pigments: a Handbook of their History and Characteristics* vol. 1, Washington: National Gallery of Art, Cambridge: Cambridge University Press.

Feller, R. L., N. Stolow, and E. H. Jones, (1985) *On Picture Varnishes and their Solvents*, Washington: National Gallery of Art.

Franks, F. (1983) *Water* (rev. edn 1984), London: Royal Society of Chemistry.

Gettens, R. J. and G. L. Stout, (1966) *Painting Materials: a Short Encyclopedia*, 2nd edn, New York: Dover Publications.

Gordon, J. E. (1968) *The New Science of Strong Materials*, Harmondsworth: Penguin.

Harley, R. D. (1980) *Artists' Pigments c. 1600–1835: a Study in Documentary Sources* (2nd edn 1982), London: Butterworth.

Hodges, H. (1964) *Artifacts – an Introduction to Early Materials and Technology* (3rd edn 1989), London: Duckworth.

Horie, C. V. (1987) *Materials for Conservation*, Sevenoaks: Butterworth.

Leigh, G. J. (1971) *Nomenclature of Inorganic Chemistry, Definitive Rules 1970* (3rd edn 1971), Oxford: Blackwell.

Long, P. and R. Levering (eds) (1979) *Paper – Art and Technology*, San Francisco: World Print Council.

Mayer, R. M. (1970) *The Artists' Handbook of Materials and Techniques*, ed. E. Smith (4th edn 1982), London: Faber & Faber.

McCrone, W. C. and J. G. Delly (1973) *The Particle Atlas*, vol. 2, Michigan: Ann Arbor Science.

McCrone, W. C., L. B. McCrone and J. G. Delly, (1978) *Polarized Light Microscopy*, Michigan: Ann Arbor Science.

Mills, J. S. and R. White (1987) *The Organic Chemistry of Museum Objects*, London: Butterworth.

Pickwoad, N. (ed.) (1986–8) papers of the 10th anniversary conference, 'New Directions in Paper Conservation', *The Paper Conservator* vols 10–12, Oxford 1986, Worcester: Institute of Paper Conservation.

Rossotti, H. (1975) *Introducing Chemistry*, Harmondsworth: Penguin.

Shields, J. (1970) *Adhesives Handbook*, London: Butterworth.

Street, A. and W. Alexander (1944) *Metals in the Service of Man* (9th edn 1989), Harmondsworth: Penguin.

Tate, J. and J. Townsend (eds) (1987) *SSCR Bulletin 9* (volume devoted to water).

Tate, J. O., N. H. Tennent and J. H. Notman (eds) (1983) *Resins in Conservation*,

Proceedings of conference held in May 1982, Edinburgh: Scottish Society for Conservation and Restoration.

Thomson, G. (1978) *The Museum Environment* (2nd edn 1987), London: Butterworth in association with International Institute for Conservation.

See also various publications of:
The Open University, Science Foundation Course, Unit S102
Royal Institute of Chemistry.

### Journals, newsletters and conference proceedings of the following organisations:

American Institute for Conservation (AIC)
Australian Institute for the Conservation of Cultural Material (AICCM)
Canadian Conservation Institute (CCI)
Institute of Paper Conservation (IPC)
International Institute for Conservation (IIC)
IIC–Canadian Group
Scottish Society for Conservation and Restoration (SSCR)
United Kingdom Institute for Conservation (UKIC)

### Journals

*AICCM Bulletin*
*The Conservator* (UKIC)
*Journal of the American Institute for Conservation*
*Journal of the IIC–Canadian Group*
*The Paper Conservator* (IPC)
*Restaurator*
*SSCR Journal*
*Studies in Conservation* (IIC)

*Art and Archaeology Technical Abstracts* (formerly *IIC Abstracts*), published semi-annually by the Getty Conservation Institute in association with the International Institute for Conservation of Historic and Artistic Works. AATA is an international abstracting journal for conservation.

The *List of Acquisitions* and *Subject Index* are published every two years by ICCROM commencing 1977.

### The Conservation Information Network

The Conservation Information Network is an international co-operative project initiated by the Documentation Program of the Getty Conservation Institute (based in California). The Network consists of a series of databases: bibliographic, conservation materials, conservation supplies and equipment databases. These are held on a mainframe computer at the offices of the Canadian Heritage Information Network in Ottawa, Canada. They are accessed using a personal computer or standard ASCII terminal and a modem through the international telecommunications system. The Network was launched in 1987 and there are over 500 individuals and institutions from around the world subscribing to it. The co-operating partners are: AATA, Conservation Analytical Laboratory of the Smithsonian Institution, ICCROM, ICOMOS, ICOM and CCI. Further information about the Network is available from:

Conservation Information Network
Communications Canada
365 Laurier Avenue West
Journal Tower South, 12th Floor
Ottawa, Ontario
Canada K1A 0C8

Within the United Kingdom, information is also available from:

The Conservation Unit
Museums & Galleries Commission
16 Queen Anne's Gate
London SW1H 9AA

# Index

# Photographic credits

1.2 A. Gallenkamp and Co Ltd; 1.3 Casella, London; 1.4 Casella, London; 2.1 Open University; 2.2 Open University; 4.18 Open University; 4.22 Open University.